Writing Philosophy Papers

FIFTH EDITION

ZACHARY SEECH
Palomar College

Australia • Brazil • Japan • Korea • Mexico • Singapore • Spain • United Kingdom • United States

To my family

Nona, Lynn, Kyle, Vanessa, Trevor, Kristi, Madeline, Todd, Randy, Evelyn, Ryan, Jamie

Writing Philosophy Papers, Fifth Edition
Zachary Seech

Acquisitions Editor: Worth Hawes

Editorial Assistant: Kamilah Lee

Marketing Manager: Christina Shea

Marketing Assistant: Mary Anne Payumo

Marketing Communications Manager: Darlene Amidon-Brent

Project Manager, Editorial Production: Samen Iqbal

Creative Director: Rob Hugel

Art Director: Maria Epes

Print Buyer: Becky Cross

Permissions Editor: Tim Sisler

Production Service: Sara Dovre Wudali, Buuji Inc.

Copy Editor: Linda Ireland

Cover Designer: Riezebos Holzbaur Design Group

Cover Image: Nick White/Digital Vision/Getty Images

Compositor: Integra

Wadsworth
10 Davis Drive
Belmont, CA 94002-3098
USA

Cengage Learning is a leading provider of customized learning solutions with office locations around the globe, including Singapore, the United Kingdom, Australia, Mexico, Brazil, and Japan. Locate your local office at **international.cengage.com/region.**

Library of Congress Control Number: 2007937153

Student Edition:
ISBN-13: 978-0-495-50684-3
ISBN-10: 0-495-50684-2

Cengage Learning products are represented in Canada by Nelson Education, Ltd.

For your course and learning solutions, visit **academic.cengage.com.**
Purchase any of our products at your local college store or at our preferred online store **www.ichapters.com.**

Printed in the United States of America
1 2 3 4 5 6 7 12 11 10 09 08

Contents

Preface

Writing Philosophy Papers goes beyond general instructions on paper writing. The whole book focuses on how to write *philosophy* papers. The kinds of papers most often assigned in philosophy classes are explained, and a whole chapter is devoted to writing the traditional philosophy paper: the thesis defense paper. Chapter 7 explains how to use specific philosophical resources, with a strong emphasis on Internet research.

Whether it's a question about organization, documentation, research, or writing style, the student will now have the answer *before* submitting a paper to the professor. This should be a relief both to the professor who reads and grades the papers and to the student who can hardly do a good job of writing a paper if the task itself is unclear. Professors assign different types of papers. *Writing Philosophy Papers* shows students that many paper assignments are hybrids of the basic kinds. In this book the students learn the basic skills, although the actual instructions for their specific classroom assignments will vary. Professors may also specify a preferred style of documentation. Footnotes and endnotes are illustrated in this book. So is the MLA parenthetical documentation. Both methods are clearly displayed in a sample paper in Appendix B. In-text citation and the number system of documentation are also explained. Documentation of Internet sources is illustrated also.

The focus is on philosophy. The many examples throughout *Writing Philosophy Papers* are from philosophical concepts or primary and secondary sources in philosophy. In addition, there is a discussion of philosophy courses, philosophical topics, philosophical reasoning, philosophy journals and research books, as well as the Internet and other research sources.

I learned to write philosophy papers from many of my former professors and also, in various ways, from my students. There are too many people to name. Nevertheless, I thank them all. My colleagues have also been very helpful. I thank the members of the Behavioral Sciences Department at Palomar College for their consistent and sincere support. I want to thank Worth Hawes, Philosophy Editor at Wadsworth Publishing Company, and Patrick Stockstill, Assistant Editor. I also thank Kammy Lee, Editorial Assistant, and Linda Ireland, copy editor. Judy Cater and Katy French helped with the library resources section. Thank you, Judy and Katy. I appreciate also the availability of Dr. Richard Lineback, Editor and Founder of the Philosopher's Information Center, and the contributions of the reviewers of the fifth edition of *Writing Philosophy Papers*: Mia Wood, Pierce College; Jorge L. Nobo, Washburn University; and Brain B. Clayton, Gonzaga University.

Finally, I express my gratitude to my family for the many times and ways they have warmed my heart and made me smile.

Zachary Seech

Introduction

We call them "papers." In college, professors require students to write papers to show how well they think and research and how well they understand and express ideas. These same professors write and publish papers of their own for the benefit of other professors and thinkers around the world.

In daily life, people often toss around ideas, collecting a little information through newspapers or magazines, voicing their own opinions and criticizing other viewpoints. But rarely do we take the time to develop our thoughts fully on a single topic. Half-baked ideas are sometimes the only items on our daily menus.

Writing a paper is a good way to develop your ideas on one topic in a thorough and precise way. You make an effort to prethink and rethink your ideas. You reword those first, faulty phrases and express your best thoughts in the best way you can. You don't know how good you are until you've done it. The result should be something you can be proud of, something that displays clear thinking and good language skills. You end up with a physical product, a set of printed pages that shows your reflective judgment on an issue. Often, the educational process generates nothing more tangible to testify to your skills.

This is an opportunity to express your ideas in an impressive way. Unfortunately, students sometimes lose this opportunity. The testimony of this loss comes in words of complaint and lament:

- The paper is due tomorrow and I haven't even started it yet.
- I have no idea what the professor wants for this paper.
- What is she going to grade on, anyway?
- I don't have the books I need, and now it's too late.
- I'm on the last page of my paper, and now I see that I can't prove what I said I would in the first part of the paper. What can I do?
- What does he mean by "argue for"?

Much of what students need to know about writing a paper goes unsaid. There is so much for the student to know and so little time for the teacher to teach the basics of paper writing. *Writing Philosophy Papers* is written to help professors advise their students on how to write a philosophy paper and to give students in philosophy classes a better chance to demonstrate their skills. If you study this book carefully, one of the frequent obstacles to learning should be largely overcome. Good luck!

1

First Things First

You have been instructed to write a paper for a philosophy course. Here is your first advice:

Start right away.

Whether the paper is due this week, next month, or two months from now, do something about it today or tomorrow. Even if you can't start the heaviest phase of your work yet, getting the project going will ease your mind. It can also give you ideas to turn over in your mind and help you plan your time. Putting off the first steps often results in a late paper, a poorly written paper, or both.

How do you start? This depends on what kind of assignment you have been given, when it is due, and how well you understand the details of the assignment.

KNOW THE ASSIGNMENT

Sometimes it is difficult to do a job well even when you know exactly what must be done. Very seldom can you do a good job when someone else sets the goal and the goal isn't clear to you.

You can't expect to write the kind of paper your professor has in mind if you don't understand what the requirements are. If you were absent or late even once, find out whether you missed any oral or written instructions. If you missed written instructions, obtain a copy. If you missed oral instructions, copy them from a student who took good notes or ask the professor. Read the instructions carefully. Reread them. Study them. Ask your questions early.

KNOW THE CRITERIA FOR EVALUATION

Be sure you understand how your work will be evaluated and graded. Here is a list of common criteria for evaluating student papers in philosophy. Your professor may use some of these criteria or all of them (perhaps applied in a different way). Your professor may also add other criteria.

- ***Choice of topic or thesis:*** Your topic or thesis should not be too broad to be covered thoroughly or too narrow to be worth covering. If you are defending a point of view, it should not be so uncontentious that hardly any reasonable person will disagree, or so far-fetched that no argument can make it seem plausible. (See Chapters 1 and 2.)
- ***Tone:*** Most assignments of college papers call for an objective tone, without inflammatory language or indignant tone. Even when you defend one view, do not sound closed-minded. (See Chapter 2.)
- ***Balance of presentation:*** When presenting information or evidence, your position is usually strengthened rather than weakened when you discuss alternative views on the issue and explain why you think it is reasonable to favor one of them. However, this criterion varies, depending on the purpose of the paper. (See Chapter 2.)
- ***Organization of paper:*** The opening paragraph usually announces the task its author undertakes, and it often previews the main parts of the paper. All transitions should be clear and smooth. The structure of the paper will depend on what type of paper is being written and the professor's special instructions. (See Chapters 2, 3, 4, and 5.)
- ***Originality:*** If there are academic sins, plagiarism is among the most damning. You plagiarize when you use another author's wording (or wording close to it) or ideas in a way that allows a reader to conclude that the words or ideas are yours. Always indicate the source of any information, thoughts, or wording that you have borrowed for use in your paper. (See Chapters 2, 4, and 8.)
- ***Accuracy:*** When presenting information or explaining someone else's views, be careful not to misrepresent. Careless wording can skew the ideas in subtle but important ways. (See Chapter 5 and Appendix A.)
- ***Use of language:*** Correct grammar and spelling are expected. Punctuation should be used correctly. Avoid unnecessarily complicated or obscure phrases and sentences, and eliminate sentence fragments. Be precise, choosing your words carefully. Always edit and rewrite your papers. (See Chapter 5 and Appendix A.)
- ***Clarity:*** In addition to clarity of organization and general language use (having clear sentences, clear paragraphs, and a logical flow of ideas), you may need to define key terms. (On defining key terms, see Chapter 2.)

- ***Consistency:*** A rushed or inattentive writer may shift positions or wording within the paper so that what is written at one point in the paper conflicts with what is written at another point. (See Chapters 2 and 4.)
- ***Strength of argumentation:*** When arguing for a thesis or point of view, offer reasons that an unbiased, clear-thinking person would find persuasive. (See Chapter 6 and Appendix C.)
- ***Research:*** Use credible sources as you put your paper together. Use enough research information to justify your claims. Your research should be thorough and relevant to your topic. (See Chapter 7.)
- ***Format:*** If a specific form for references, page setup (including margins and font), and presentation of your paper is designated, follow that form. If your topic seems to justify a departure from the assigned format, consult the professor before writing the paper. (See Chapter 8 and Appendix B.)
- ***Neatness:*** Papers should be clean, with few if any handwritten edits on white computer-printed paper. The back of the sheet of paper should be blank. Computer preparation is almost always required. If the paper is handwritten, it must be easily readable and have no scratched-out words.

These criteria may vary in importance, depending on the professor and the assignment. In some cases, a glaring weakness in only one of these categories will be enough to drop your overall grade below passing. For example, if your grammar or the strength of your argumentation is very poor, you may not receive a passing grade, no matter how well you accomplish some of the other tasks. *Before* you start writing, be sure you know how the professor will evaluate your work.

SCHEDULE YOUR TIME

After you are sure you understand the assignment and how it will be evaluated, you should break the project down into specific tasks and set a deadline for each of them. This will enable you to work at an effective pace.

As you write out your schedule, take into consideration your other school and nonschool obligations, the availability of resources like computers and hard-to-get books, and the due dates of the paper and any preliminary submissions you are required to make. Don't schedule your tasks so tightly that unforeseen personal emergencies will prevent you from completing the paper on time.

Try scheduling *backward* from the final due date (and any fixed dates for an outline, a rough draft, or other work that must be submitted). Ask yourself how many days you probably need—not the minimum you need if all goes well—to type, edit, and proofread a final copy. Write a target date on your schedule. Now continue scheduling backward. Write dates for the following sorts of things: your final rough draft; a first complete draft; a first draft of each major part of the paper; a revised outline; completion of Internet, library, or other research; preparation of a first outline; topic selection. When you are done you may find that you do not have as much time as you want. There is usually no choice except to go back to your schedule and compress it. Even when you are working under strict time constraints, some peace of mind comes from knowing you have a schedule that will allow you to complete the paper on time.

Some of your tasks might be delayed by circumstances beyond your control. Get to those things early. You can apply at your academic or public library for interlibrary loans for books from other libraries, but the books may take weeks to arrive. Scheduled interviews are sometimes canceled. Computers to which other people have access are sometimes unavailable when you need them. Finally, some books and articles yield slow reading, and some kinds of research are time-consuming.

Here is a sample of a short schedule. The dates indicate when each part of the project should be completed.

Feb. 4:	Topic selection
Feb. 24:	Outline
Mar. 8:	Rough draft
Mar. 18:	Final copy

You can also plan your intended workdays and the tasks for each day. Here is a sample of a more detailed schedule for the same project.

Feb. 2:	Spend day in library checking on topics
Feb. 4:	Select topic
Feb. 5:	Look for resources; apply for interlibrary loans
Feb. 7–13:	No time to work on paper this week!
Feb. 14:	Do research, 2–4 PM
Feb. 16–21:	Do research and write outline
Feb. 24:	Revise outline and write
Feb. 28:	Write
Mar. 5–8:	Write and revise
Mar. 8:	Finish rough draft
Mar. 11, 13:	Revise
Mar. 14, 15:	Print and proofread
Mar. 16:	Review and revise
Mar. 18:	Print and proofread
Mar. 20:	Due date!

Post your neatly written, printed, or computer-printed schedule where you will see it every day. As the days or weeks pass, record the *actual* completion date for that task in the margin next to each item. If you fall behind by more than a few days, you may have to revise your schedule.

TYPES OF PHILOSOPHY PAPERS

The papers assigned in philosophy classes are usually **thesis defense papers.** The purpose of a thesis defense paper is to state a position and give reasons for believing it is true. For example, you might, on an issue in ethics, claim that "Major corporations have a moral obligation to repair the environmental damage they have done." Reliable evidence and strong reasoning are at the heart of a good thesis defense paper. Chapter 2 focuses specifically on thesis defense papers.

Other kinds of papers are sometimes assigned. The purpose of **compare-and-contrast-papers** is to show how two views, books, articles, or philosophies are alike and how they differ. The purpose of **research papers** is to survey important views that have been published on a certain topic. The purpose of **summary papers** is to restate someone else's views in your own words. **Explanatory papers** go beyond summary to illuminate the views with analogies, examples, or comparisons. These kinds of papers, and some hybrids of them, are discussed in Chapter 3.

With the exception of the research paper, each of these kinds of papers—thesis defense, compare-and-contrast, summary, and explanatory—corresponds to a certain type of essay question that a professor may give to students on a take-home or an in-class test. So, even if you have not been assigned all of these kinds of papers, you may benefit from reading these parts of this short book.

PHILOSOPHY COURSES AND SAMPLE PAPER TOPICS

Most Introduction to Philosophy courses provide some instruction in ethics, metaphysics, and epistemology. Sometimes political philosophy and philosophy of religion are included in the introductory course. For your paper, you should probably choose a topic that relates to material that has been presented in the class. Get the professor's approval before working on a topic that relates only indirectly to course readings and lectures. In some cases, the professor will assign a topic or hand out a list of acceptable topics.

Most other philosophy courses, at either the undergraduate or the graduate level, focus on one area within philosophy. Here are descriptions of several areas of philosophy and some sample paper topics for courses in these areas. (These topic phrases may serve as titles of papers. They are not theses. A thesis is stated in sentence form.)

- ***Ethics:*** *The study of moral rights and responsibilities.* Sample topics: Why corporations have moral obligations; A morally justifiable national policy on abortion; A utilitarian justification of universal mental health insurance; Who is responsible to care for AIDS patients?; Two views of Kant's moral imperative.
- ***Political philosophy:*** *The study of political rights and obligations; the study of social justice.* Sample topics: What should a person do when conscience conflicts with law?; Martin Luther King, Jr.'s concept of a just law; Who should feed and house the homeless?; Hobbes's state of nature and contemporary international law; The relationship of John Locke's views on human nature to his views on a fair society; Human rights and civil rights.
- ***Metaphysics:*** *The study of theories of reality.* Sample topics: Quantitative and qualitative accounts of nature in the pre-Socratic philosophers; Ancient and modern atomism; Must metaphysics be scientific?
- ***Epistemology:*** *The study of how humans can know, the kinds of knowledge, and the possibility of certainty.* Sample topics: Circularity in Descartes's *Meditations;* The subjectivity of scientific knowledge; Levels of certainty.
- ***Philosophy of religion:*** *The study of problems of knowledge and truth in religion.* Sample topics: Can empirical evidence prove the existence of God?; Concepts of the divine; Rational and irrational elements in prayer; R. M. Hare's concept of faith; Minds and souls.

There are also other areas of philosophy such as: *Aesthetics,* the study of art and beauty; *Philosophy of science,* the study of fundamental concepts and paradigms in the sciences; *Philosophy of mind* and *Cognitive science,* which explore influences between consciousness, brain processes, and conceptualization; *Philosophy of history,* the study of principles that structure social history; and *Logic,* the study of formal relations between truths.

In *Critical Thinking* courses, we study the dynamics of good reasoning in practical settings such as everyday conversation and public media communications. Papers in critical thinking courses (and some logic courses) may examine reasoning skills directly. They may also be thesis defense papers on topics of general interest, in which the student is instructed to *demonstrate* critical thinking skills.

Topics should not be so broad that they can't be examined thoroughly, or at least convincingly. "Plato" is too broad a topic. "Plato's ethics" is still too broad. Entire books can be dedicated to this vast topic. "The three-part soul in Plato's *Republic*" is a more workable topic, and you may have to get even more specific than this. You may narrow it down to "the relation between the four cardinal virtues and the three-part soul in Plato's *Republic*" or even focus on only one of those virtues (e.g., temperance).

Topics should be worth writing about. They should be interesting and illuminating, yielding sufficient discussion to warrant a paper. For example, a paper on how frequently a philosopher uses a certain word or expression is not worth the effort unless this inquiry somehow contributes to a more significant issue.

WHAT YOU WILL FIND IN THIS BOOK

In Chapter 2, you will encounter some basic concepts of writing papers and a detailed discussion of thesis defense papers, the most commonly assigned kind of paper in college philosophy classes. In Chapter 3, you will learn about the other kinds of papers mentioned earlier. You should read about thesis defense papers, even if you have been assigned a different kind of paper. Often, those other kinds turn out to be variant forms of the basic thesis defense paper.

In later chapters, you will find hints on how to write and edit your paper. Research skills are also explained both for general resources and for those that are specific to the field of philosophy. Unless your professor instructs otherwise, your references—notes, works cited—should be in a standard format. The formats most frequently used in philosophy are illustrated in the sample citations in Chapter 8.

If you haven't done so already, look at the table of contents for this book. You will get a good idea of what sorts of help the book will afford you, and an overview of the text allows you to reference specific sections of the chapters quickly.

Good luck with your paper. Be sure you "make" most of that luck by doing your best work. Again, call to mind the opening advice:

Start right away.

2

Thesis Defense Papers

The **thesis defense paper,** sometimes called an argumentative paper, is the kind most often assigned in college philosophy classes. The paper topic may be one that deals with academic issues in philosophy. However, because philosophy courses on ethics may address not only the ideas of philosophers but also everyday issues and contemporary events, papers in those courses may not seem to be on "philosophy" in any technical sense. Also, because logic, which is one area of philosophy, aims at the improvement of basic and generic reasoning skills on any issue, papers for logic and for critical thinking classes may focus on many sorts of topics in current affairs, human nature, and everyday life. So thesis defense papers for philosophy classes may be of three types, according to subject matter: pure philosophy, applied philosophy, and general topics.

In a thesis defense paper, you make a claim and give good reasons for believing that it is true. You defend your claim as you argue that much better reasons exist for accepting it than for rejecting it. You may not be able to prove beyond all doubt that your thesis is true, but you should try to show that an unbiased, clear-thinking person would have good reason to accept it.

DEVELOPING A THESIS

Thesis comes from an ancient Greek word that means *stand* or *position.* Your thesis is the stand or position you take on an issue. In a thesis defense paper, you generally state your thesis at the beginning of the paper and then spend the remaining paragraphs and pages showing why that position is correct or reasonable.

A topic, like abortion, is not a thesis. A thesis is always given in sentence form and a position is taken on the topic. Although "abortion" is not a thesis, the following statement *is* a thesis: Abortion is morally wrong in all cases, except when the mother's life can be saved by aborting a nonviable fetus. This also is a thesis: Abortion of a fetus in the first trimester of pregnancy is the moral right of the woman. If you ask yourself a specific question about your topic, your answer to the specific question may serve as a thesis. In the preceding examples, the question would have been, "Under what conditions is abortion morally permissible?" Here are a few more sample theses:

The existence of God cannot be established through empirical evidence.

The charge that Descartes's second and fifth Meditations display circular reasoning rests on a misunderstanding of his concept of God.

The charge that Socrates criticized others' ideas but never offered ideas of his own is false. He offered a constructive philosophy of the morally justifiable life. (Note: The thesis is stated in two sentences here, but it articulates a single idea.)

A course in Religions of the World should be required for all secondary school students.

Choose a thesis that is worth the effort you will put into arguing for it. A position that hardly anyone would seriously disagree with, or an arguable position on a trivial issue, is not worth your time. You don't want to make your point, only to be met with a shrug of boredom: "So what?"

On the other hand, a very broad thesis may turn out to be too difficult to support. (Reread the comments on topic breadth on page 6 in Chapter 1, if you do not remember them clearly.) A paper on a grand topic achieves little for its author if the thesis has not been shown to be plausible. To show this, you need at least one good line of reasoning that rests on evidence from reliable sources. You may need to begin by working with a tentative thesis and search to find if supporting evidence is available. You may find after research that the opposing thesis is more defensible than the one tentatively selected!

Don't close your mind by staying with your first idea for a thesis, even after you see that you would have to suppress some evidence and overplay other evidence in order to defend it. Consider arguing for the opposing thesis instead, or rewording the thesis to make it more defensible.

Occasionally, professors assign a specific thesis (or "thesis statement") for a paper. If this is not the case, you may be assigned one or more general topics from which to develop a thesis. For example, if the class will be reading René Descartes's *Meditations,* the professor may assign a paper on the topic of Methodical Doubt (a method of inquiry which is displayed throughout the six Meditations, but most obviously in the first Meditation), or the topic of the "cogito" argument—roughly, "I think, therefore I am" (from the second Meditation). On the first topic, you may claim in your thesis statement that Descartes does not consistently apply his own method, or you may claim that this method is appropriate for establishing some kinds of knowledge but not all kinds. On the second topic, you may claim in your thesis statement that the philosopher's reasoning is faulty, or you may claim that he is unclear about some aspect of the inference (e.g., the concept of self or thought). Notice that, from each general topic, there may be various specific thesis statements that you can develop.

Often, you will not even be assigned general topics for your paper. You may simply be instructed, for example, to write a paper on Descartes's *Meditations.* As you develop a thesis about a particular philosopher's ideas, ask yourself how you would honestly evaluate the supporting reasoning if someone else—someone whose ideas you respect—were to present similar ideas to you in personal conversation. (Of course, sometimes the ideas are so complicated or foreign that this is difficult to imagine.) The basic idea that will form the core of your thesis does not have to be complicated. After you explain in writing, thoroughly and with precision, the details and implications of your idea, your paper may be longer than you expected.

You will generally not be asked to come up with a completely original idea—that is, one that no one has ever ventured before. It is sufficient if the idea is original to you—it is one that you have thought of on your own. In some cases, the professor will not even mind if the observations are ones you have read about elsewhere, as long as the observations are expressed in your own words and your sources are acknowledged.

THE OPENING AND CLOSING PARAGRAPHS

Most philosophy papers have an introductory paragraph. Many also have a finalizing paragraph to provide closure. Professors' preferences on these vary. If you have no specific instructions concerning this from the professor, include at least an opening paragraph. (Short summary or explanatory papers are likely exceptions.)

There are two kinds of opening paragraphs. The first is a *formal* kind that helps the reader anticipate the reasoning that will be offered in the paper. To write this kind of introduction to your paper, make two things clear to the reader in the very first paragraph: precisely what your thesis is and how you intend to support it. Here is an example of an opening paragraph from a thesis defense paper:

> Animal experimentation is necessary in the search for cures for human diseases, even though it sometimes causes pain and even death to the animals. Four basic points, to be argued for in this paper, lead to this conclusion. First, humans generally have a greater obligation to preserve human life than to preserve animal life. Second, some cures cannot be discovered in any other way. Third, despite popular misconception, very few of these experimental projects do in fact cause serious harm to the animals. Fourth, some of the experiments give us information about the animal species that ultimately is used to protect individuals of that species or the species itself.

Although four "basic points" are previewed in the sample paragraph, your paper may have as few as two supporting lines of reasoning to be developed, or as many as six or seven. It is better to have fewer fully explained points than several that are not well thought out. The thesis statement is not always the first sentence of the opening paragraph. The preceding paragraph, for example, could have been introduced with one or more sentences describing the public controversy on this issue. (In a variation on this formal opening paragraph, the introduction identifies the major sections of the paper rather than the basic points of support. One section may present background information; another may present a defense against a counterargument; yet another may draw out implications or the social significance of the thesis.)

The second kind of opening paragraph, called *rhetorical*, introduces the topic by discussing its importance, and perhaps its timeliness. Background information on the topic may be provided. In this way the writer motivates the reader to read on. (A rhetorical opening paragraph is not overstated or emotionally unrestrained. A later section, "Tone," will explain the language style that is appropriate for most college papers.) The thesis is stated but the supporting arguments are not necessarily previewed. Here is an example of this kind of opening paragraph:

> Few people doubt that nonhuman animals can experience pain and some sort of emotional distress. Morally mature people will not cause unnecessary anguish for sentient beings. Modern science can, however, make valuable advances through animal experimentation. The moral dilemma that results is a serious one, and it has recently been a subject of impassioned social discourse. Although we should not judge lightly, one conclusion is compelling. Animal experimentation is necessary and justified in the search for cures for human diseases, although it sometimes causes pain and even death to the animals.

Avoid platitudes and excessively broad generalizations. Don't claim as common knowledge views that are actually contentious. Be precise, saying exactly what you mean. (See the discussion, "Precision of Expression," on pages 37–40 in Chapter 5.)

If your professor does not assign one of these kinds of openings, you may choose for yourself.

There are two kinds of closing paragraphs. They parallel the kinds of openings. In the "formal" closing paragraph, the author usually restates the thesis and reviews the main arguments. Thus, it mirrors the opening paragraph. Here is a sample closing paragraph from a thesis defense paper:

> It has been argued in this paper that we have a greater obligation to preserve human life than animal life, that some cures cannot be developed by other means, that animal experimentation usually does not seriously harm the animals, and that the animal species itself can benefit from some of this research. These points lead to the conclusion that animal experimentation is necessary in the search for cures for human diseases, despite the animal pain and death sometimes involved.

When writing a formal closing paragraph, always go back to the opening paragraph to ensure that you are now claiming to have done just what you promised, and refer to the rest of the paper to ensure that this is what you did establish. Sometimes an author establishes a worthy position in the paper but begins and/or ends with a thesis statement that is both grander and more difficult to support. What a shame. Now the author has not established the claim made in the thesis statement. This weakens the paper. Pay attention to the wording of the opening and closing paragraphs. Have you done what you said you would do? (The section on "Consistency" in this chapter and the section on "Precision of Expression" in Chapter 5 offer more to think about concerning the importance of careful wording.)

If you do not use a formal style in closing, you have two alternatives. You may simply end without any closing remarks at all (assuming this is not an abrupt and therefore awkward ending), or you may close by remarking on the general topic or the importance of the view you have defended. Here is a closing paragraph of this kind:

> We should not allow the public discussion of animal experimentation to go on without resolution. Responsible animal experimentation for medical reasons is well-justified. Scientists in this field deserve to be recognized as socially responsible researchers, rather than to be challenged as moral outlaws. Moreover, public funding of such research should not be constantly imperiled because of the sensitive character of the issue.

THE BODY OF THE PAPER

The body of the paper is everything between the opening and closing paragraphs. The structure of the body of a thesis defense paper should reflect the preview in the opening paragraph, if you have written a formal opening. Assume the sample formal opening paragraph from the preceding section is your opening paragraph. Then in the next group of paragraphs (perhaps set off by the roman numeral I) you should present reasons for believing that humans have a greater obligation to preserve human life than animal life. After you make your best case for that, in the following group of paragraphs (continue the roman numerals if you started them in the preceding section), you should give reasons for believing that some cures for human diseases cannot be discovered in other ways. The third (III) group of paragraphs should display the best reasoning you can offer for thinking that most animal experimentation causes little harm to the animals. The final (IV) group of paragraphs should support your final point: in this case, that animals themselves are sometimes aided by this research. (A point like this last one, which is not essential to your line of reasoning, should be included only if you can support it convincingly. You weaken your paper whenever you offer poorly supported opinion.)

The reader should know what you are trying to do in each part of the paper and how that relates to your conclusion, the thesis statement. Don't let the reader think, "I wonder what point this author is driving at?" If the structure of the body of your paper reflects your opening paragraph preview (covering the same matters in the same order), and if your closing paragraph is in keeping with both of these, the reader will be able to follow your reasoning more easily than if you make the reader read through part of the paper before figuring out what you're up to.

Make it even easier than that. When you shift from one point to another, use transition phrases to call attention to the shift. You can write, for example, "The second main argument in support of the thesis of this paper is that . . ." Or you can write, "The next step in the line of reasoning that supports the thesis of this paper . . ." As mentioned earlier, you can also divide your paper into sections with roman numerals or even titles to help the reader keep track of your points and recall how they relate to your thesis. If an intelligent, attentive reader is confused when reading the paper, you need to make it clearer. Providing good, clear reasoning is the author's job in a thesis defense paper. The discussion in Chapter 6, "Good Reasoning," is designed to help you do your job well.

Making clear shifts between sections and letting the reader know what you are up to are even more important if you have written a rhetorical rather than a formal opening paragraph because the structure of the paper has not been previewed for the reader.

Paper writers are often tempted to include side issues that are related to the general topic but tangential to the thesis. The rule on what to include in your thesis defense paper is clear. If it provides necessary background or is part of the planned support for the thesis, include it. If it is just an interesting tangent, exclude it. The purpose of your comments in the body of the paper is to support the thesis statement. Delete discussions that belong in "another paper."

ARGUING FOR THE THESIS

The author of a thesis defense paper argues for the claim that was made in the thesis statement. That thesis statement, remember, expresses the assertion that the author intends to establish as true or probably true. But notice the use of the word *argue:* the author "argues" for the claim.

In everyday discourse, people commonly use the word argue to describe heated, contentious advocacy of an idea. This popular use of the expression may mislead in a discussion of thesis defense papers and reasoning in philosophy generally. In these cases, when someone says you must *argue, present an argument,* or *defend a thesis,* there is no intention to suggest that you are supposed to narrow your mind, become an angry adversary, or oversimplify. Instead, you are supposed to present well-reasoned thoughts about why the thesis is a credible one and to base your reasoning on good evidence. Your paper is weakened if it sounds as if you are wearing blinders. Philosophers, as much as thinkers in any other academic discipline, pride themselves on fairness in appraising even unpopular points of view, and the thesis defense paper is where we expect that this will be done in a careful and thorough way. Now consider some pointers on how to make a respectable argument for your thesis.

Tone

Don't allow yourself to sound like the worst stereotypes of politicians and advertisers. Don't try to sell your ideas with overblown rhetoric. Are you convinced by the politician or advertiser who obviously exaggerates the strengths of the favored view and the weaknesses of the disfavored one? No. Instead, you get the impression that persuasion is more important than accuracy and fairness to this opinionated or unprincipled advocate. You wouldn't be surprised to learn that supposedly factual claims were just fabricated.

This way of selling an idea or product won't work in academic writing either. The reader of your paper looks for good reasoning and reliable insights. It's a mistake to think that the author strengthens a thesis defense paper by wielding heavy-handed language or empty rhetoric. Sounding sure of yourself isn't the same as sounding reasonable, and the professor is unlikely to confuse the two.

An open-minded writer does not fabricate facts or play up evidence as if it establishes more than it actually does, so avoid the unrestrained language that suggests you might do this. An open-minded writer does not treat other views unfairly, so avoid undisciplined expressions that suggest that you are not above such contrivance. In a paper advocating a pro-choice position on abortion, don't refer to "anyone so foolish and insensitive to think that a woman has no right whatsoever over her own body." In a paper advocating a pro-life position on abortion, don't refer to "the degenerates who feel that their personal convenience is more important than a human life."

You earn credibility by the tone of your wording. If you sound as if you listen to reason rather than jump to conclusions, the reader has no reason to believe you are closed-minded. Your ideas will receive a better hearing. If you avoid extreme language that smacks of indignation, self-righteousness, and derision, the reader has no reason to discount what you have said before you finish your argument.

Premises, Conclusions, and Transitions

A reader may confuse the author's premises and conclusions if these are not carefully distinguished. A *premise* is any statement of evidence—that is, any observation or claim that is offered in support of the point to be proven. A *conclusion* is any statement for which evidence has been offered.

Clearly, your thesis statement is a conclusion. The purpose of a thesis defense paper is the presentation of evidence for that statement. You will probably have other conclusions in your paper as well. The several main points that together are meant to demonstrate the truth of your thesis-conclusion will almost certainly be supported by further specific evidence. Thus, the statements that directly support the thesis-conclusion are both premises (because they constitute the reasons for believing the thesis) and conclusions (because evidence is presented for those statements). You can think of your thesis as the *ultimate conclusion*. It is supported then by *transitional conclusions* that are both premise and conclusion, enabling you to make a transition from your secondary argumentation to your primary one.

The primary argumentation is the move from the transitional conclusions to the ultimate conclusion or thesis statement.

For an example, consider the line of reasoning illustrated in the preceding sections, "The Opening and Closing Paragraphs" and "The Body of the Paper." The thesis and ultimate conclusion, fully stated, was "Animal experimentation is necessary in the search for cures for human diseases, even though it sometimes causes pain and even death to the animals." The four transitional conclusions previewed in the formal opening paragraph were the "four basic points to be argued for in this paper." These are supported one at a time in the body of the paper with the best evidence the author can supply. A good paper has both a clear structure and compelling evidence.

When you shift between stating evidence and conclusion (whether transitional or ultimate), you should make the shift very clear. Moves that are obvious to you because you already know what you intended to say may be unclear to a reader. So make good use of *conclusion indicators* and *premise indicators.*

Conclusion indicators are expressions that often precede and serve to announce a conclusion. *So, thus, therefore,* and *consequently* are words that perform this function. In addition, there is the less common *hence* and innumerable phrases such as *this leads us to the conclusion that* and *it follows that.*

Premise indicators are expressions that often precede and serve to announce a premise. *Since* and *because* are the most common premise indicators in both spoken and written English. Various phrases like *due to the fact that* and *for the following reasons* also introduce premises.

You can also use entire sentences to signal major shifts from one argument to another. You might write, for example, "We have now considered the evidence for the first of the three main points to be offered in support of the thesis that private individuals should not be allowed to possess handguns or semiautomatic weapons. Let us move on to the second point." In this case, a pair of sentences proclaims a shift that no attentive reader can miss.

The reader should not only be able to understand the sentence being read but also know how you intend to relate it to the sentences and paragraphs around it and in the rest of the paper.

Presenting Other Sides

Thesis defense papers sometimes include a special feature: counterarguments—that is, reasoning that goes against the point of view expressed in the thesis of the paper. There are two kinds of counterarguments. Some are arguments that a critic might level directly at your thesis without attention to the specific supporting arguments that you have offered in support of your thesis. Other counterarguments are arguments that a critic might use to discredit one of the specific lines of reasoning with which you have supported your thesis.

Why would you include arguments against the point of view you have adopted? After all, the purpose of the thesis defense paper is to present the strongest case *for* your thesis, and the rule on what to include in the paper dictates that only what supports the thesis statement merits inclusion.

The answer is that you do strengthen your case by giving voice to counterarguments *if* you can respond to these concerns with good reasoning. By demonstrating that you have anticipated the concerns of people who would critique your views, you can avoid giving the reader the sense that you are smugly self-assured and thoroughly unappreciative of other perspectives on the issue. When you fail to bring up a likely objection to your position or your reasoning, you allow the reader to conclude that you simply do not have a good answer to it—or that you are unaware of it. A good answer can neutralize that objection in the reader's mind and allow your own arguments to be more persuasive.

It does you no good to make up weak counterarguments that insightful critics would never employ. The objections that you anticipate in your paper should be credible ones. They can be critical comments that you have come up with on your own, noting what others may perceive as weak points. You might introduce such a critique by writing, "A critic may object to this line of reasoning on the following grounds." Then you explain the concern and respond to it. On the other hand, the objections may be ones that have actually been offered by others in the face of views similar to yours. You can introduce them in this sort of way: "Professor Moreno has objected to this kind of argument in her book *Social Fallacies* by saying . . ." You can also think of an objection of the kind that would probably be pursued by a particular thinker. For example, you might write, "A. J. Ayer would almost certainly object to this argument because it is based on . . ." In such a case, you would project from the writings of that author to a specific argument of your own. Be sure you do not misrepresent the views of that author. When you respond, do not sound intolerant and do not oversimplify the concern. If it is a sufficiently important counterargument to be included in your paper, then it will deserve respectful attention. If the objection has some merit, you can acknowledge that without "giving away the farm"—that is, without conceding all aspects of the critique.

If you intend to include one or more counterarguments to your position or reasoning, consider announcing your intention in the opening paragraph. Of course, if the contended point is a relatively minor aspect of your reasoning, the counterargument may not warrant opening-paragraph status.

Consistency

If you don't pay enough attention to *how you word* the claims you make in the paper, your language will be imprecise. It will sound sloppy, especially to a professor, who is used to precision in her or his specialty field of study and research.

Language is precise when it actually expresses what you intend and what you can justify. In daily life, we often say what we don't really mean. We say, for instance, that our favorite soccer player "didn't do a thing right on the field today," when that claim is false because, despite an exceptional number of errors and misjudgments on the field, he sometimes—even frequently—dribbled and passed the ball effectively. He probably did many other things "right" also. We stretch the truth through exaggeration. In our haste, we choose words or phrases that are roughly like, but still dissimilar from, those we *should* choose.

Thus, it should not be surprising if we are also imprecise when we write academic papers. This imprecision is especially problematic when we word the thesis in a significantly (though perhaps subtly) different way as we restate it later in the paper. For example, let's consider a sample thesis that was mentioned earlier in this chapter:

> The existence of God cannot be established through empirical evidence.

Note first that the adjective "empirical" refers to experience of physical objects through the five senses of humans. After the initial (opening paragraph) statement of the thesis, a hasty author might offer its restatement as "God cannot be known," or as "There is no reason to believe in God." Although the original thesis might justifiably be offered as partial evidence for these other claims, these claims *are* different from the thesis itself. They are not simply different wordings of the thesis. It may be that the original thesis is true, while the two "restatements," which actually go beyond the original claim, are false. Keep in mind *exactly* what you had claimed you would demonstrate in the paper. Don't let the thesis wander. The attentive reader of your paper (your professor, in this case) will wonder: Which of these points *does* the writer intend to establish? Evidence that is relevant to one of the forms of the thesis may not be relevant to the others.

3

Special Kinds of Papers

Thesis defense papers are the kind of assignment for which philosophy classes are known. They call for the sorts of reasoning skills and conceptual analyses that are at the heart of philosophy. Thesis defense papers are not the only kind of written work assigned in philosophy classes, however. Many professors assign work that is subtly or even strikingly different from the assignments of their neighboring professors.

In this chapter, because of the wide spectrum of assignments for papers, we examine other basic kinds of papers that are assigned in philosophy classrooms. These are:

- Compare-and-contrast papers
- Research papers
- Summary papers and abstracts
- Explanatory papers

Even if you have been assigned one of the kinds of papers that is dealt with specifically in this chapter and you have not been assigned a thesis defense paper, do read Chapter 2 on thesis defense papers. Some of the general pointers about paper writing are covered there. Furthermore, as you will soon discover, both the compare-and-contrast papers and the research papers are often best presented in a thesis defense format. Even in summary papers and explanatory papers, you will often have to identify the thesis and argumentation of the writer whose work is being described.

COMPARE-AND-CONTRAST PAPERS

In any written assignment, you should pay attention to the verbs used in the description of your task. The words *explain, analyze, identify, compare, contrast, illustrate, summarize, locate, arrange, justify, define, prove, describe,* and *recount* refer to different sorts of tasks. Each is used to ask you to do something different. The wording of an assignment sometimes includes more than one of these expressions. In these cases, you must be especially careful to read attentively, distinguish all the terms from one another, and perform each of the assigned tasks.

One common kind of paper is the **compare-and-contrast paper.** Students may be asked to compare and contrast (1) the ideas of specific philosophers named by the professor, (2) the ideas of any philosophers in a particular philosophical movement, with the selection made by the student, (3) philosophical movements or schools of thought, (4) specific books by different authors, (5) specific books by the same author, and (6) the ways that one concept is developed in different times, by different thinkers or groups of thinkers. Examine an example of each of these:

Compare and contrast the political views of John Locke and Thomas Hobbes.

Compare and contrast the ethical thought of one utilitarian and one intuitionist.

Compare and contrast logical positivism and ordinary language philosophy.

Compare and contrast *The Trial* by Franz Kafka and *The Castle* by Albert Camus.

Compare and contrast Plato's *Charmides* and his *Laches*.

Compare and contrast the concept of utopia as developed by St. Thomas More and by Edward Bellamy.

The sort of subject exemplified by the last of these is often easiest to address because it specifies both the topic and the thinkers, thus limiting the range of material you must synthesize and analyze. Notice that the first of the examples would have been much more specific if it were of this sort. The instructions might have read: Compare and contrast the concepts of a social or political state of nature as developed by John Locke and Thomas Hobbes.

The search for comparisons and contrasts is, of course, nothing more than an attempt to find what is similar and what is different about the two things being compared. Many of the dissimilarities will be obvious. If you are familiar with the things to be compared, you will almost certainly notice some things that can be said of one but not the other. If you do not discern differences, you probably need to do more reading to familiarize yourself with the details of the ideas involved in the assignment.

The similarities may be more difficult to recognize. If you do discover that the two things you have to compare seem to have little in common, try thinking about very general aspects. Perhaps the thinkers or philosophies that are being compared share at least some unstated assumptions about human motivation, political rights, mental capacities, language, emotion, personal fulfillment, or some other important notions relevant to the comparison. The things being compared almost always have something in common, some point of agreement or similarity.

What will provide a focus for the compare-and-contrast paper? In what way will the paper hang together and be grasped as a unity by the reader, rather than read just as a series of comments on various similarities and dissimilarities?

(A compare-and-contrast paper should be more than a listing of views.) One way of providing such unity is to preview your comparative paper with a short account of the general ways that the compared things are the same and the general ways that they are different. Generalize and give an overview of your assessment.

When you do this, you almost transform this kind of paper into a thesis defense paper like the ones described in Chapter 2. You might profitably take the extra step and create a thesis statement, completing the transformation. In the thesis statement you should proclaim your assessment, saying generally how the two things being compared are similar and how they are not. While some compare-and-contrast papers are not written in an explicit thesis defense format, your professor may require it and, even if it is not required, it may turn out to be a useful way to organize and present your paper. Consider several sample statements:

> Plato's ideal society as presented in the *Republic* and Edward Bellamy's as presented in *Looking Backward* share several definitive assumptions about the character of good citizens and healthy relations between social groups, but they diverge significantly on desirable political structures and styles of living.

> Plato and Bellamy agree that social conditions greatly influence the character of interactions in a society, but they disagree on the extent to which divergent individual traits can be changed.

> Plato and Bellamy share the belief that personal wealth and acquisitiveness must be controlled in any society that is to avoid corruption, but they differ on which social policies could bring about such a change in people and on whether such a change could be universal.

The remainder of the paper's opening paragraph may preview the sorts of evidence to be offered. Then the philosophers' general positions and specific passages from their writings can be offered as evidence for—as reasons for believing—each of these claims. If you do not word your compare-and-contrast paper as a thesis defense, there is another structural issue to consider. Should you, in the first half of the paper, deal with one of the two things to be compared, and then compare and contrast as you present the parallel aspects of the second? Or should you move back and forth between the two, comparing one aspect of each at a time?

Generally, the second of these approaches is better. Why? With the first approach, you don't engage the reader immediately in the activity of comparing and contrasting, which is both engaging and the purpose of the paper. The reading is more likely to be tedious. Also, with the first approach, you may make it necessary for some readers to continually return to the first part of the paper to remember what you wrote there about each aspect that is being considered in the second part. This is awkward and irksome. If you do lots of reminding in the second part in order to avoid this problem, you become redundant. That can be bothersome too.

One hybrid approach calls for a short summary of each of the two things to be compared, followed by a comparative section. It is hard to do this well. Short summaries do not give a basis for an in-depth comparison, and long summaries are tedious and require that the heart of the paper be deferred to the end.

Despite the generalizations made here, each of these structures for a compare-and-contrast paper may be more workable than the others for a certain topic. Do not make a final decision on the paper's structure until you consider what it will take to deal with the specific material and highlight the desired points.

RESEARCH PAPERS

A research paper is any paper for which you must locate and examine information from multiple sources, especially "secondary" sources (which will be explained later in this section). The specific sources to be used may be indicated in the professor's wording of the assignment. Usually they are not; you are expected to identify and find relevant resources on your own.

Research papers normally sandwich the body of the paper between an introduction and a closing paragraph, as most other kinds of papers do. However, there are additional parts to a research paper. You must have a final page or set of pages that is titled "Works Cited" or "Bibliography." A Works Cited section displays information such as author, publisher, and date of publication—or Internet site information—for each source to which you referred in your paper. The correct way to record this information is explained in Chapter 8.

The Works Cited section is sometimes titled "Bibliography" (or "Works Consulted"), especially when you want to include works that were helpful to you but to which you did not actually refer in the paper. (Works may refer not only to books and articles but also to musical scores, speech texts, and nonprint sources like video, audio, and electronic productions.) Occasionally, a paper includes a list of cited works as well as a bibliography of other sources that were consulted and contributed to the author's general understanding of the topics addressed. Sometimes a section titled "Endnotes" (or just "Notes") is included. This is for the commentary notes and references to sources that would have been footnotes if they had been placed at the bottom of pages rather than in that Endnotes section. These references are numbered with a superscript—a number raised above the regular level of the type—in the text of the paper and at the beginning of each note. Generally, a paper will have a format that employs either endnotes or parenthetical references to a Works Cited list through the text, but not both. See Chapter 8 for more on these formats. Research papers sometimes also have a section called an "Appendix." Here you place a graph, chart, document, or explanation that is too extensive, or perhaps too incidental, to include in the body of the paper, but which the reader may find useful. If more than a single appendix is attached, they should be designated "Appendix A," "Appendix B," and so on. The appendixes are placed before the Endnotes and the Works Cited or Bibliography pages. Finally, the bibliographic section may be annotated—that is, each work listed may be described briefly. The annotation is usually no more than several sentences or a paragraph long.

Of course, compare-and-contrast papers may involve some, or even much, research. Certainly a research paper may also have a thesis defense structure—in fact, it usually does. The papers assigned in college philosophy classes are often combinations of the simple types described in this book. The research for a philosophy paper is generally library research and/or Internet research.

Often, however, these searches can be augmented by contacts you can make with people in the field about which you are writing. People who are reliable authorities can give you worthwhile testimony of their own or refer you to other sources. For example, the author of a paper on environmental policies might consult officials in the U.S. Department of the Interior or recognized naturalists. The author of a paper on relationships between mind and body might consult a chemistry professor, a scholarly physician, or a scientist working in that subfield. The author of a paper on the philosophy of sport might find helpful a conversation with coaches or athletes in professional sports or in Olympic competition.

Modern technology has made research easier. With computer cataloging, for example, digging for information in the library is a quicker and surer task than it has ever been. However, the greatest impact of technology on scholarly research is that much of the source-hunting and analysis is now accomplished online from personal home and office computers. This is true for both student scholars and for veteran scholars with advanced academic degrees. In Chapter 7 you can learn about research skills and sources for inquiry into general and philosophic subjects.

Your research paper may involve both *primary sources* and *secondary sources*. Primary sources are books or articles that are a writer's original work—perhaps in translation, however, from another language—on a subject about which you are writing a paper. Secondary sources are books or articles *about* the philosopher or book or article that is a primary source. An example will help. Gilbert Ryle wrote a book titled *The Concept of Mind.* If your paper is on Ryle, reductionism, mental processes, or Ryle's book itself, then this can be a primary source for your paper. If you find an article by someone else, reviewing and evaluating Ryle, or even a section of a book in which Ryle's ideas in *The Concept of Mind* are summarized, you have a secondary source for that paper. For some assignments, students are asked to read only primary source material. Often they are expected to use both primary and secondary sources. Seldom is a paper to be forged only from secondary sources.

SUMMARY PAPERS AND EXPLANATORY PAPERS

Students may be instructed to summarize or paraphrase the first of Descartes's six *Meditations*. They may be instructed to summarize John Stuart Mill's *Utilitarianism,* William James's essay *Pragmatism,* or one or more of the twelve parts of David Hume's *Dialogues Concerning Natural Religion*. With this sort of assignment, the professor intends to evaluate the students' understanding of the philosopher's position and arguments, rather than to evaluate their ability to offer their own critique of those ideas. These may be called **summary papers**. Such overviews, which are often relatively brief, are frequently not referred to as "papers" at all.

Do not begin to write a summary of a philosophic text—or any other text, for that matter—before you have finished reading it. Why? A summary is not intended to be a sentence-by-sentence rewriting of the original. It is not intended even to have the same number of paragraphs as the original. Often, the opening paragraphs do not get to the heart of the matter. They may be introductory and even incidental to the main argument. You need to know where the author is going, what the thesis and main lines of reasoning are. Idiosyncrasies of that author's style of writing or presentation should not show in your summary. Therefore, you need to know the entire passage to be summarized before you begin writing. A peculiar or self-indulgent style may be the right of the author of the original passage, but a summary should be clear and focused and should not draw attention to *its* author. So don't just change the turns of phrase or use synonyms to alter the word choice. You can pack that author's ideas into much less space because you are presenting only the essentials of that document. Some students attempt to rewrite individual sentences without understanding what the author is up to, and that understanding is precisely what your professor wants to confirm. For specifics on how to phrase your writing, avoiding stiff wording and common errors, read on through Chapter 5.

Don't expect to be able to articulate perfectly the views of a philosopher after a single reading. Even several readings may be insufficient if you are reading straight through the book, chapter, or article as if it were part of a novel. In academics, where subtle differences in wording can be crucial (and the writing style is sometimes frustrating!), we—both students and professors—usually have to study paragraphs, not just read them. We constantly ask questions like, "How does this sentence relate to the preceding or following one?" and "What did that long sentence (that I just read) with so many clauses mean?" We keep stopping to reread sentences and ask if we still are clear about what the author is trying to prove and how one point is meant to support another. Outline what you read, take notes, and see whether you can compose an abstract. An abstract is an extremely brief summary of one to several paragraphs, stating the thesis and main lines of argument. It is somewhat like a good opening paragraph and only slightly more detailed.

You may find that even when you are not asked to write a summary paper on some writing you must master, it may be worth the effort for your own purposes. Composing an abstract or summary paper clarifies the author's argumentation in your own mind, and it provides a tool for reviewing that written piece and recalling it after time has passed and you have been distracted by chemistry classes, psychology classes, and everyday life.

In **explanatory papers**, you may go beyond summary to explain the author's reasoning and views by *adding* points you have crafted to illuminate that author's intention. An analogy, for example, might be used.

> Descartes, in his *Meditations,* resolved to find a single point of certainty, then to draw conclusions, one at a time, that follow necessarily from the preceding points. This is similar to the inferential process of geometrical proofs, in which we move from what we know or postulate to other relationships which must necessarily be true if the initial ones are.

In a simple summary, the analogy to geometry would not be included, since Descartes does not, in the *Meditations*, discuss the geometrical model of reasoning directly. In an explanatory paper, however, the writer may offer this analogy to illuminate the reasoning process described and applied by Descartes.

The writer may also employ examples to illustrate the author's points.

> The character Socrates in Plato's *Republic* claims that an unjust or unhealthy soul has conflict between its elements, such as a conflict between a person's Reason and Appetite. To envision such internal strife, we might think of meals at which we eat that extra helping of food, when our reason tells us we shouldn't because of the extra calories or the bloated feeling that will result.

The writer may also help the reader of the paper understand a point or its role in the thought of the philosopher by commenting on the relationships between the work being explained and another work of that philosopher, or by comparing or contrasting it with the work of another philosopher. In addition, references to the life or cultural context of the philosopher may be useful. These are a few of the elements that might be included in an explanatory paper to bring the material to be explained into sharper focus.

You may encounter other writing projects in philosophy classes also. Journals and notebooks are sometimes assigned. Both the content and the format of these vary so widely that guidelines on writing them cannot be ventured here. The professor who assigns the work will provide instructions. Finally, you may be asked to write a reaction paper. In a reaction paper, you express subjective reactions to the material that you have read. Justification is usually not required. You may choose to report on any personal reaction, emotional or intellectual.

4

Writing and Revising the Paper

Start right away.

This was the advice you received on the first page of Chapter 1. You were told that you should make sure you understand the assignment and the criteria for evaluation. You were told to make a work schedule for the paper and to plan interlibrary loans, interviews, computer access, and reading time so you don't run out of time at the end. This is all good advice. But don't slip into self-deception as you spend time on these preparatory activities. Don't keep busy with the planning, researching, and organizing while you put off the actual writing until the last minute. It is very common to delay the writing with the belief (or rationalization) that, even halfway to the due date for the paper, you are just "not ready to write yet." Although you do need to gather information, develop a tentative thesis, and plan the body of your paper, you should also consider the *start right away* advice to apply to the writing too.

Even if you have to start with very subjective preresearch paragraphs related to the topic you are investigating, start within a week of receiving the assignment (earlier if you have less than a couple weeks to the due date) and write something. Perhaps you won't use your early musings in your final draft, or even in your first full rough draft, but it will help you refine your thinking on the topics you are considering, and it is likely that you will end up with ideas to keep and develop as well as sentences and paragraphs to discard. This prewriting may take as little as fifteen minutes a day.

In this chapter, we review the first steps in forming a paper: choosing a topic, gathering information, and shaping a thesis. We also cover another preparatory step, outlining. Then we get to the writing itself. We discuss the rough and final drafts that any well-developed paper goes through. We also discuss writing style. There is some discussion about computer word processing, which focuses on the development, formatting, and printing of a paper.

GETTING STARTED

Let's review the initial steps for creating a paper. If a specific paper topic has not been assigned, you must decide on a subject. Sometimes you will get an idea that sounds great but is unworkable because the supporting evidence and arguments that were expected to be available are not. Your research does not yield the needed kind or amount of information. Or your anticipated lines of reasoning are not convincing when they are put down on paper. This happens to the best of professional writers, so don't let it lead you to the conclusion that you are on track for failure. These false starts are part of the business of writing. (Last-minute composition, when you do not have time for false starts, compounds the frustration.)

If you are allowed to choose your topic, try to settle on one that genuinely interests you. When you choose a topic that was mentioned as an example in class, but in which you have no personal interest, writing a paper soon becomes tedious. Besides, people tend to write better papers when their enthusiasm amplifies their energies and sharpens their thinking. Having to be thorough and precise is demanding even when the topic is one for which you have an affinity. You set yourself up for mediocrity if you select a topic that bores you even before you start writing.

Should you try to select a topic and then gather information on it to find whether it is workable, or should you do some exploratory reading in the library in order to settle on a topic? The answer is that it varies with topics, assignments, and writers. Sometimes you know right away just what you would like to write on, sometimes you have a general idea, and sometimes you don't have a clue. However, assuming that you are employing a thesis defense structure, take care not to become inflexible about your thesis. Look up the relevant sources of information to see if you can make a good case for the thesis that you are considering. If your thesis is not defensible as you have worded it, change the wording. If this is not enough, change your stand on the issue, or change the thesis altogether while you stay with the same topic. If this thesis is also unworkable, or if you have other reasons for not wanting to defend this new thesis, change topics and begin the search for a thesis again. Even if your paper is not a thesis defense, this kind of flexibility during the investigation of the topic helps you decide on your specific focus on the topic.

As you progress far into the writing of the paper, you may find that even subtle adjustments to the wording of the thesis—or adjustments to the focus of the paper—may be required. If you read an essay question on a test and fail to recheck the wording of the question, you may either answer a slightly different question or give only a partial answer to the question. Similarly, when you are feeling rushed and write the body of the paper without sufficient attention to the relation of the thesis to its support, the result will be a bungled project. The paper will be weak and perhaps unpassable. Revise that thesis as often as you have to!

MAPPING AND OUTLINING

A planning outline of a paper provides a plan that enables you to envision the entire project as intended before you write the first full-length draft. This outline displays what you expect to be the skeleton of the paper, with the main points and subpoints laid out clearly in relation to each other and to the rest of the paper. The planning outline is fashioned as you do your early research. It can guide your continuing research and argumentation, reminding you where you need more supporting evidence and helping you assess the strength of the overall argument.

Even before putting together the planning outline, you can prethink the argumentation to be used in the paper, especially if it has a thesis defense structure. (Remember that compare-and-contrast papers and research papers often have a thesis defense structure.) As you ponder the strongest ways to argue for your tentative thesis, map out these lines of reasoning by drawing a downward arrow from evidence to conclusion. You begin your map of the projected reasoning by writing the thesis near the bottom of a clean sheet of paper. For each separate reason for believing the conclusion, write that reason somewhere above the conclusion and draw a downward arrow to the thesis. If one reason for believing the conclusion (the thesis statement) has to be stated with several sentences, draw a plus sign (+) between those sentences, bracket them all, and then draw the downward arrow. For example, the thesis, still in rough form, that you are considering may be "Euthanasia for unconscious or mentally impaired patients should be decided by the patient's family." You begin by writing this in the lower section of a sheet of paper. You then ask yourself why this might be a good proposal. This thought occurs to you: The family knows the patient's character and wishes better than anyone. You reflect for a moment, then add the word *usually:* The patient's family usually knows the patient's character and wishes better than anyone. You write this above the thesis statement, but to the left so you have space to add other reasons. You draw a downward arrow from that sentence to the thesis statement. You reflect again. It is also the family that bears most of the consequences of the decision. After all, they are the ones to deal with the emotional effects of the daily absence of that person from their lives. And the people who are affected most, you reason, should make the decision. These reasons are written in toward the right of the previous one, and another downward arrow is drawn. The map of this initial reasoning is shown in Figure 1.

The plus sign between the two sentences on the right, along with the bracket that groups them, shows that these two work together to establish *a single reason* for believing the conclusion is true. They combine to make one point; each shows why the other sentence is relevant. So they have one arrow for the one inference. The arrow on the left represents a different inference: the one about knowing how the patient would feel about the situation and what the patient would want.

You can carry this mapping further. If you want to record some reasons for believing that any of the top three sentences are true, you can write those

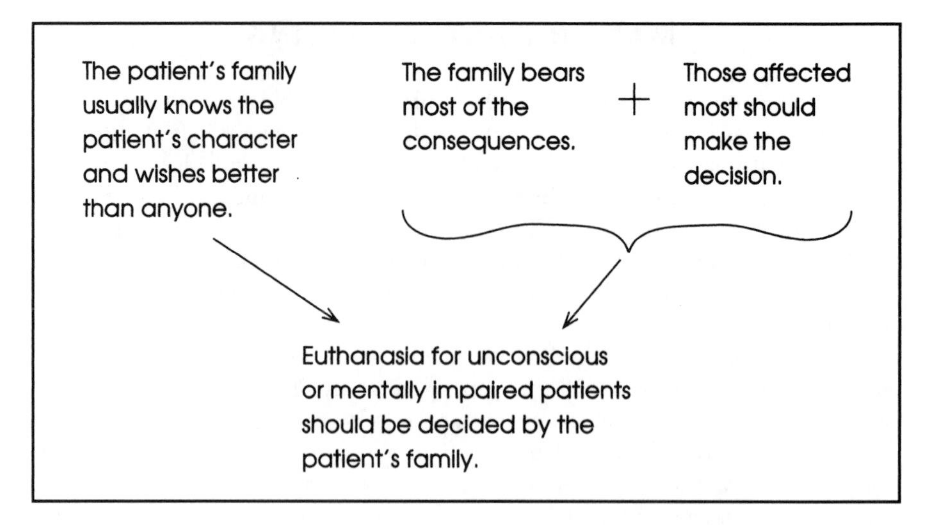

FIGURE 1

reasons above and draw an arrow down to that sentence. An extensive map can provide you with everything that you would place in an outline. You can go straight from the map to the outline and have the structure of your paper established.*

Two more points should be made about mapping your reasoning. First, it is fine to do early maps by abbreviating sentences rather than writing them out. "Family bears consequences" is sufficient to remind you of your point. Second, maps are useful during the working stage as well. When you are researching and revising your reasoning, maps can help you visualize the current state of your argument so you can continue to work without losing track of the big picture.

An outline may be written with either full sentences or phrases. Using an outline, you can structure your paper before you write it. A thorough outline often designates each paragraph in the paper. In traditional formal outlines, the main sections of the paper—opening paragraph, closing paragraph, and each main point in the body of the paper—are labeled with roman numerals. Each of these sections is divided into at least two sections labeled with capital Arabic letters. Each of these, in turn, is divided into at least two sections, labeled with numbers. Further subdivisions are marked with lowercase Arabic letters. The following illustration may help.

* For a detailed explanation of this kind of mapping, see *Open Minds and Everyday Reasoning*, 2nd ed. (Belmont, CA: Wadsworth, 2005), by Zachary Seech

I. Opening (formal) paragraph
   A. Thesis statement
   B. Main points to be argued for in support of the thesis
      1. Point one
      2. Point two
      3. Point three
II. First main point (same as I B1)
   A. First topic under II
      1. First topic under A
      2. Second topic under A
   B. Second topic under II
   C. Third topic under II
III. Second main point (same as I B2)
   A. First topic under III
   B. Second topic under III
IV. Third main point (same as I B3)
   A. 1.
         a.
         b.
      2.
   B.
V. Closing (formal) paragraph
   A. Restatement of thesis
   B. Restatement of main points supporting the thesis
      1.
      2.
      3.

As you can see from this illustration, you may have more than two divisions in a category (e.g., A, B, C; 1, 2, 3; a, b, c, d), and it is acceptable to have one item in a level subdivided (e.g., A) although another item of the same level (e.g., B) is not.

The planning outline becomes a working outline as you allow yourself to alter parts of it throughout the process of researching and writing the paper. Sometimes you find that you cannot argue effectively for one of the claims in your outline. You then have to change the claim, replace that argument, or delete it. Sometimes you decide that the paper needs to be reorganized because what you originally placed as a subheading under heading III fits better under IV. Occasionally, you may conclude that what had seemed important to include in the paper really adds little or no strength to the overall argument. It may be an interesting tangent that doesn't belong in the paper at all.

There may be no need for a final outline. A final outline is a working outline that has been revised to show all the changes that were made, even if they were made as you transcribed the final draft. Final outlines are usually composed only when the class assignment requires an outline to be submitted with the paper. When this is required, the outline should be placed immediately after the cover sheet unless the professor instructs otherwise.

ROUGH AND FINAL DRAFTS

Don't let your first draft be your last draft. Nobody writes that well. Some people are surprised when they discover that even great authors revise, rewrite, and edit their work, and that this can be really difficult and sometimes frustrating work for them. Writing comes from the mind and often the heart. These are not the same in any two people. So what you write will be different from what another person would write on the same subject. Still, to do the best writing you can do, you have to prethink, write, rethink, and rewrite. With careful attention to your own work, you will find discrepancies between what you wrote and what you meant. Or you will find that your first thoughts are not your best thoughts. Maybe you write well enough to get an acceptable grade on fewer rewrites than it would take to do your best work, but it's only your best work—or something close to it—that you can feel really proud of when you put your name on the cover sheet.

Authors of college papers (and others) may delay the writing stage—which, you remember, should start early—because they fear their writing will not be good. So they acquire a sort of writer's block. They are unable to start writing. One cure to try if you are afflicted with such a malady is this: *Give yourself permission to write poorly!* That means you should let yourself put words down on paper without thinking about whether the result will be something you are willing to share with another person—if that is what it takes to get you started. Decide that, after writing one page, you will read it over and then choose whether to roll the paper up in a ball and toss it in the trash basket. If you do toss it, no one will have seen your words except you. You can start over on that day or another as if it were the first time. However, the chances are good that some ideas, sentences, or turns of phrase will be worth keeping. If nothing else, you will learn about some dead ends, and this will leave you with a better notion of how to approach the subject the next time. And you will have started writing. It's a way to break the ice if you are experiencing a cold spell (not only when you start writing, but at any point in your project).

You need multiple drafts to finish with your best work. By starting early, you give yourself time between drafts. If you read what you have written immediately after writing it, separating the ideas you wanted to convey from the paragraphs you have written may be difficult. As you reread your own writing, you might be thinking not only of what the words would actually convey to a reader but also the additional feelings and unarticulated associations that you had in mind when you wrote the words. You may not notice that you need *more words* or *different words* to convey all of what you had in mind. Generally, more time between drafts allows you to get a better perspective on what you have actually said in your writing.

As you revise your early drafts, you can consider changing the order in which your thoughts are presented. You can consider whether some material that has been written in should be excluded and whether any new sections, paragraphs, or sentences should be included. You can check to see if more transition statements ought to be added and whether the transitions that you have already written are clear and helpful to the reader. The paper may be easier both to write and to reorganize if you construct it from notes that you have made on three-by-five-inch cards. You can change the order of the cards as you decide on the order in which your points should be made. If you also write the bibliographic information for your sources on these cards (see Chapter 8), your reference citations will be easier to write later.

When you edit for a final draft, check for spelling, grammar, and phrasing. Even if you are good at editing your own paper, you should have at least one other person who is also good at editing read your paper and offer recommendations. You know what you meant in the first place and may tend to see a "correct" reading, overlooking errors that would be obvious to another reader. For the same reason you should have someone else proofread it if possible, checking primarily for typographical errors.

Here is a proofreading hint: when proofreading either your own or someone else's writing *for spelling rather than for meaning*, start by reading the last word in the paper first, then read the next to the last word, and continue in this direction until you finish at the beginning of the paper. This method prevents the proofreader from seeing what is expected rather than what is on the page. When proofreading *for meaning rather than spelling*, it sometimes helps to hear the sentences read aloud. A sentence that is structured awkwardly or that misstates an intended point may be more obvious than if it were read silently. It may also help to have someone else read it to you at least once. Since the reader is not familiar with your intended wording, a confusing sentence structure may trip up the fluency of the reader and announce to you the need for restatement.

In its final form the paper is typed on a computer and double spaced, unless the professor instructs otherwise. It must be done neatly. Ideally, there are no inked or penciled alterations. There should never be many, and they should all be small alterations, such as the insertion of a missing letter in a word. Normally, the left and right margins are one to one-and-a-quarter inches, and the top and bottom margins are each about one inch. Figure 2 displays a standard format for the cover page. Professors' instructions vary. You may be asked to include or exclude a cover page, or it may be optional. You may be asked to bind the pages of the paper with a staple or with a paper clip. Plastic or paper binders or report covers may be allowed or disallowed.

PLAGIARISM

The word *plagiarism* comes from a Latin word that means *plunderer* or *thief.* Writers plagiarize when they present others' words or ideas without making it clear that these are not their own words or ideas. The price for plagiarism can be high. In scholarly writing by professionals, the price may be an irreversible loss of

Character Roles in the Platonic Dialogues

Mariana Rios

Ancient Greek Philosophy
Philosophy 3105
Dominican University
March 13, 2008

FIGURE 2

reputation, and even censure by professional organizations. In colleges and universities, student writers may face a failing grade on the assignment, a failing grade in the course, academic probation by the school, or even expulsion from the school.

Make sure you have not plagiarized. Check each of the phrases or ideas you borrowed from other sources to see if you have credited the source. For a direct quotation, use quotation marks and announce the speaker or writer and also the resource from which the quote came, using one of the methods described in Chapter 8. If you paraphrase, credit sources in the same way. If you acquired a general idea from another source, you can indicate this in the text of your paper or with a comment note located at the bottom of the page or at the end of the paper.

Professors recognize writing styles, word usage, and distinctive claims that alert them to the possibility or probability that a source was not credited. They are likely to notice (a) when the author of a paper has failed to acknowledge one of several sources researched, and also (b) when a paper has been purchased from an advertised "service" informally known as a "paper mill." In addition to their time-honed skills of detection, professors now have online programs for identifying plagiarized passages. Detection is frequent and the academic price—failing the course or expulsion from the school—is high. The desperate student who is buying the paper "just this once" often reassesses the situation and regrets the misjudgment too late. Even the "custom" papers that are supposedly crafted for unique assignments are identifiable. To avoid the pricey oops of unintended plagiarism, students now can use computerized programs to check their own writing. For example, some schools subscribe to programs like Turnitin, and then make the service available to students.

Remember: Acknowledgment of the source is what distinguishes a scholar from a plagiarist. Finally, be clear and specific in your acknowledgment, so the reader can know the extent to which the material has been borrowed. One endnote marker at the end of a paragraph may not be enough to tell the reader how much of the preceding was not original.

RESPONDING TO CRITICISM

You will probably be blind to some of the weaknesses of your own paper. Some language errors or peculiarities, some omissions, and certain logical fallacies that can be quickly spotted by an astute reader may elude you even after you have reread your writing several times. The problem, of course, is that the writing is your own. The ideas are your own. You already know what you intended to say, and *that* (what you intended to say) is what comes to mind when you review the words you used. For almost every writer, the critical comments of others can help in improving a piece of writing.

Ask someone to read your writing and make *specific* recommendations for improvement. Then pay attention to those comments. Take them seriously. In some courses, the professor or another student will provide this critical perspective. (*Critical* means evaluative, not negative.) The usefulness of this constructive criticism depends in part on how you handle it.

Don't become defensive. Most of us respond too quickly with counter-arguments when someone tells us that our views—or even the wording of our views—should be revised. If you cannot control your emotions, if you become angry at the critic or feel overwhelmed, you will find it difficult to recognize when good points are being made. Remember that, even when the critic is missing part of your point or is being a bit abrupt, there may be something for you to learn. You might not agree with all the critical comments you encounter. (Who does?!) What a shame, however, if you miss the germ of helpful insight that was incorporated in, or suggested by, the general criticism you rejected. Often, reading comments on your own writing will yield new ideas about how to revise your paper—ideas only indirectly suggested by the critic.

As you have more and more of your work reviewed and critiqued by others, try to increase your capacity to learn from it. When you do decide to change a word, phrase, example, or line of reasoning, choose wording that makes sense both to you and to others. This will not necessarily be the alternate wording (if any was offered) that was proposed by the critic. The paper is still yours, and the wording should be yours while you work to make your meaning clear to careful readers.

Sections of Chapter 5—"Precision of Expression," "Overstatement," "Vagueness," and "Definition"—as well as Chapter 6 and the examples of revision in Appendix A to this book should help you focus on ways to improve your writing.

WRITING STYLE

You wouldn't write a memo like a novel and you wouldn't write a short story like a technical manual. Different kinds of writing have different functions. Your writing style should be adapted to the purpose. It should also reflect the audience you are addressing. You wouldn't write a children's book using the same language that you would use if you were addressing professional anthropologists or attorneys.

When you write a college paper, the primary and sometimes sole reader is the professor of the course for which the paper is written. One common mistake in writing papers is to omit information about a philosopher or philosophical movement because "the professor already knows that." You should explain such things because the professor wants to know whether *you* know the material well enough to characterize it with precision and because your paper should be a topical essay that would have the same persuasive force if read by others. *Write as if you were explaining your topic to an intelligent adult with little or no background in academic philosophy.* Imagine yourself writing for a biologist, psychologist, or computer analyst. Do not condescend or use a very simple vocabulary, but do not assume that the reader (even though it may be the professor) knows that you understand the basics of the issue. There are exceptions to this rule. In advanced philosophy courses, you can use philosophical terms like *epistemology* and *metaphysics* with no explanation and even make comparative references to other philosophers, theories, or movements without describing their views.

Some people write very stiffly. That is, their writing sounds awkward because they feel that a paper calls for a rather formal kind of expression, but their version of formality obscures rather than clarifies. Their sentences may be long, with lengthy and confusing clauses. The grammar may be bad because even they get lost in the structure of the sentences they write. They may use words incorrectly and include words they do not normally use and have not mastered. Many of these people speak quite lucidly. If you ask what they meant in one of those unclear phrases, they may be able to tell you straightforwardly and immediately. These people need to write more like they talk. This doesn't mean that all writers should write the way they talk or even that these people should write *exactly* the way they talk. People who have this problem should, however, listen to themselves articulate a point orally in a simple way before committing it to paper. Perhaps the written sentence will require more precision, but listening to the directness of oral expression may be a good start as they try to undo their misconceptions about academic communication.

Other people need the opposite advice. They should try to stop writing the way they talk. Generally, these are people who write in such an informal, everyday colloquial manner that vagueness obscures points and the trendy or folksy flavor of the writing is distracting.

Strive for a paper that is both readable and precise. Say exactly what you mean but say it as clearly as possible. Remember to maintain a tone of open-mindedness, intimating a broad perspective despite the quite specific claims and arguments you make in support of one view.

WORD PROCESSING TOOLS

Don't believe them: your spellchecker, your grammar check, your thesaurus. At least, don't accept their suggestions uncritically. (In *Microsoft Word*, you find these features under "Tools" on the top tool bar.) Their sometimes helpful hints must be assessed by a writer or proofreader who has good language skills. Responsibility for what is on the page rests with the person who is named on the cover page as author of the paper.

A *spellchecker* enables you to identify any words in the document that are not in the built-in lexicon. Of course, this does not enable you to identify problems caused by typing in the wrong word. For example, if you mistakenly typed "male" instead of "mail," the spellchecker would not alert you to this fact because both are in its list of recognized words. The spellchecker will also challenge any word that is not in its lexicon, even though the word may be spelled correctly. Many of the technical terms used in philosophical studies (e.g., "sorites" and "noumenal") and names of philosophers (e.g., "Unamuno" and "Rorty") will be flagged.

Although a *grammar check* may indeed announce to the writer an error to be corrected, it may also propose an unwarranted change that would introduce grammatical error into what had actually been correct text. Do not blindly follow the advice of your word processor's grammar check.

The *thesaurus* lists words with similar meanings to one that has been highlighted by the writer. This feature also must be used with attentive caution and a good ear. There are very few complete synonyms (words with the same meaning) in the English language. Some of what is signified or connoted by one word will fail to carry over to a listed synonym, and the second word will have associations that the first doesn't. Thus, you should choose only words with which you are familiar to replace your originally selected word. A synonym in one context may not be synonymous in another.

Other tools on Microsoft Word that you might find useful are the outline feature, the dual-color text feature, and the hidden notes feature. Above all, remember to "back up" your work. Free online services provide a way to save your writing so that it is not inaccessible if your computer is damaged or otherwise unavailable. If you have a web-based e-mail service, you can "save" the writing by attaching it to an e-mail that you send to yourself!

Be watchful for editing residue. Sometimes when writers return to a passage in order to change a word or phrase, they add without deleting everything that has to be deleted. In our haste, most of us have occasionally done this. Always reread the entire sentence that has been altered, even when the change has been minor.

Finally, remember that last-minute computer problems, and the even more frequent printer problems, do occur. When this happens to you, you may feel that this reason for not submitting an assignment on time warrants special consideration from the professor. However, it is likely that the professor hears about such problems frequently. You should not be surprised if your circumstances seem less exceptional from that perspective.

5

Language

Being able to say precisely what you mean, orally or in writing, is an important communication skill. Graduates of colleges and universities are expected to display consistent proficiency in communication. Language mastery is a basic skill that, added to technical expertise in the field, enables a well-educated person to communicate both established and new ideas in one or more areas of study. Much of higher education focuses on the development of the language skills involved in concept analysis, and this is one of the primary reasons that papers are assigned, critiqued, and graded in college courses.

PRECISION OF EXPRESSION

The language and content of written work are not separable. Of course, aspects like spelling and punctuation can be critiqued separately from the ideas themselves. Phrasing and word choice, however, are not separable from meaning. Subtle changes in wording significantly alter the claims that are made. This can then alter the truth of the claims and the evidence needed to support the change. Inattention to wording, or a more basic lack of sensitivity to language, leaves you saying what you don't mean or what you cannot justify. Think about what you mean to say, then say what you mean! You will not have "said" anything except what the words convey.

Overstatement

Writers as well as speakers sometimes make bolder and less supportable claims than they should. They may do this partly because of their zeal for the general idea that they are putting into words. They may also have a habitually sloppy approach to language. Nearly everyone at least occasionally inflates language and exaggerates claims.

In informal everyday dialogue, overstatement is commonplace. "Everyone in the whole school gets along so well," claims a satisfied parent of a public school student. The parent may dismiss a counterexample or two that may be issued in challenge, maintaining that it is really true that "everyone" gets along well. The overstatement may be considered by that parent and by others to be quite acceptable, and the challenger may be thought of as nit-picking. Conversational exaggeration of this sort is frequent and generally harmless.

Habit of overstatement spills over, however, to both informal and formal discussions of politics. A liberal may say that political conservatives "never have any concern about the poor in this country." A conservative may say that liberals "are all irresponsible in dealing with the nation's finances." These broad generalizations, with the words *never* and *all*, invite us to overlook the variety of people who warrant each of these classifications. For good examples of claims that are indefensible because they are not appropriately qualified, we can simply read or listen to some political campaign rhetoric, or read certain newspaper columnists, especially on those hot political and social themes. The habit of overstatement also spills over into our dealings in business and conversations at home. It shows up where it hurts, from job applications to rumor-passing to interactions between professionals of all sorts.

Because most of us have acquired the habit of overstatement to some extent, it is not surprising that it shows up in the writing of college papers, where precision of expression and rational defense of one's claims are required.

Whether you are wording the thesis itself or constructing a line of argument to support it, choose your words carefully. Don't write "Abortion is the same as murder" if you mean that all abortions are murders or if you mean that abortion fits nearly any general definition of murder. Abortion and murder are *not the same*, after all, since murder has a broader definition. Not all murders are abortions. Don't write "Existentialists do not care about theory" if you mean that most existentialists believe that theorizing rather than reflection that results in action has been the focus of philosophy for too long. You could also then note that much theoretical work was done by those we call existentialists.

Some poorly stated claims, like the preceding one about existentialism, are simple misstatements as much as overstatements.

Vagueness

Your writing is vague when it is too general for your readers. The information or claims are not sufficiently specific. If readers are likely to respond, "But that doesn't tell me enough," then your writing is vague.

Vagueness depends on audience and context. A single description of a disease may be suitable for a layperson's guide to illness, but it may be extremely vague in a pathology article for physicians. Vague answers are often intentional and acceptable in casual conversation. They are sometimes offered in purposeful efforts to avoid giving specific information—perhaps to spare someone's feelings. In an academic paper, however, vagueness is seldom appropriate. Thinking of your reader as an intelligent nonphilosopher, or at the most as someone who is familiar with basic philosophical terms and views, you should work on being specific in your writing as you lay out evidence and argument.

There is not a sharp line of demarcation between statements or descriptions that are vague and ones that are not. It is easier to say whether one statement is less vague than another. Because a vague paper is not a well-written one, strive to be specific as consistently as you can. In a paper on the pre-Socratic philosopher Thales, the statement, "Thales believed water to be the basic stuff of the universe," could be made more specific by writing, "Thales believed water to be the source of all other materials in the world." In a paper on Plato, the statement, "The forms were ideas, but not anybody's in particular," could be fashioned into a clearer, more specific one by writing, "The forms were mental entities with an existence independent of any individual thinker." In a paper on the concept of the state of nature in the seventeenth century, the statement, "Hobbes thought everybody always acts selfishly," would be less likely to be misunderstood if it were written, "Hobbes thought that even the cooperative efforts of individuals in society could be explained by their wanting to maintain the security of organized society."

Of course, the statements that were examined and revised in the preceding paragraph might not have required the same sort of revision in the actual paper. Some of the vagueness might have been cleared up in other sentences in the passages from which they were drawn. We considered these sentences out of their context (an entire paper or paragraph). Some of the vagueness in the examples, however, was not dependent on the context they might have been set in. At the very least, precision of expression would help many readers understand the point better.

Definition

When an important word or phrase in your paper means something different when used by different people, you should define the expression to clarify how *you* are using it. For example, in a paper in which you discuss whether various traditional arguments for the existence of God are sound, you should define "God." Some of the traditional arguments establish at most the existence of a powerful creative entity, not the God that most Christians have in mind. For example, the first cause argument, the prime mover argument, and the teleological argument do not establish the existence of a Christian sort of God unless it can also be demonstrated that this first cause, prime mover, or world designer had the same characteristics as the God of Christianity. Therefore, it is important to define the term and measure your success according to the definition you have chosen to work with and share with your readers.

Any expressions that may be understood in a way different from the one you intend should be defined if the difference has an effect on whether the evidence and argument offered in the paper are compelling. By "communism" do you mean the political systems that were formerly in place in Eastern Europe, the Soviet Union, and China? Or do you mean a theoretical utopia of shared resources that has never been realized on a large scale? By "self-interest" do you mean egotistical preoccupation with oneself or do you include the prudent advancement of one's own benefit without neglect of others? Terms as basic as "human nature," "idea," "free will," "rights," "essence," "responsibility," "art," "consequences," "substance," and "belief" can be used differently in philosophical systems from the way they are used in everyday discourse. They can also be used differently from one philosophical system to another.

After you have defined an expression, be consistent in your own use of it. Be wary of *equivocation;* this occurs when you shift from one meaning of a term to another without acknowledging the shift, just as if there had been no shift. Equivocation is dangerous because it can create the impression that a conclusion follows from the evidence when it really doesn't. In a paper on free will, "free" may be used in one paragraph to indicate lack of physical restraint, in another paragraph to indicate ability to do anything one wishes, and in the conclusion or thesis it may mean psychological freedom, the possibility of choosing differently in identical circumstances. Observations about freedom that seem to lead to the conclusion may actually rest on different meanings; these observations may only appear to be related to the conclusion if we fail to distinguish between the different meanings of the word.

GRAMMAR

In college, any written work you have prepared at home for submission to the class or the professor is expected to be grammatically correct. This book cannot provide you with the kind of thorough review you can find in one of the standard guides to grammar, such as *Rules of Thumb* by Jay Silverman, Elaine Hughes, and Diana Roberts Wienbroer (New York: McGraw-Hill, 2006); however, the following observations will remind you of some basics that should not be violated.

Complete Sentences

Always use complete sentences (with a subject and main verb) except in those rare cases in which you intentionally fashion a sentence fragment for stylistic effect. Conversational patterns of discourse sometimes lead writers to present a partial sentence as if it were a complete sentence.

Wrong: Descartes resolved to doubt everything that was doubtable. Which led him to an extreme, though counterfeit, skepticism in the first Meditation.

Right: Descartes resolved to doubt everything that was doubtable, which led him to an extreme, though counterfeit, skepticism in the first Meditation.

Also right: Descartes resolved to doubt everything that was doubtable. This led him to an extreme, though counterfeit, skepticism in the first Meditation.

The dependent clause that was set off as a separate sentence in the wrong version is joined with the main clause in the first correction and becomes a proper independent sentence in the second correction.

Sometimes two sentences that should be separate are joined into one cumbersome and faulty sentence.

> ***Wrong:*** Descartes resolved to doubt everything that was doubtable this led him to an extreme, though counterfeit, skepticism in the first Meditation.

> ***Also wrong:*** Descartes resolved to doubt everything that was doubtable, this led him to an extreme, though counterfeit, skepticism in the first Meditation.

In the first of the two preceding examples, there is no separator to mark off one sentence from the other. In the second example, a comma is used, but it is not a strong enough separator to mark off one complete thought from another. An alternative is to meld the two ideas so they constitute a single thought. For example, you could write: "Descartes's resolve to doubt everything that was doubtable led him to an extreme, though counterfeit, skepticism in the first Meditation."

Agreement between Parts of a Sentence

The subject and main verb of a sentence must agree in number, and all pronouns should agree in number with their antecedents. In other words, subject and verb as well as pronoun and antecedent should match up, both being singular or both being plural.

The agreement of subject and verb is basic in our sentence structures and usually poses no problem for college students. One tricky case, however, is a sentence with two subjects, one of which is singular while the other is plural, when the subjects are joined by "or" or "nor." Should you use a singular or plural verb form? Generally, the verb form should match the nearer subject.

> ***Wrong:*** Either the Greek philosopher Pythagoras or the later Pythagoreans was responsible for the now famous Pythagorean theorem.

> ***Right:*** Either the Greek philosopher Pythagoras or the later Pythagoreans were responsible for the now famous Pythagorean theorem.

> ***Also right:*** Either the later Pythagoreans or the Greek philosopher Pythagoras, their founder, was responsible for the now famous Pythagorean theory.

In the two acceptable forms, the verb is singular or plural to match the nearer subject, the singular "Pythagoras" or the plural "Pythagoreans." Another undesirable form would display a plural verb that is nearer to the subject "Pythagoras."

Confusion can be caused by nouns or pronouns that occur between the subject and verb (that is, by phrases that modify the subject).

> ***Wrong:*** The complexity of Nietzsche's interwoven themes frustrate some readers.

> ***Right:*** The complexity of Nietzsche's interwoven themes frustrates some readers.

"Complexity" is singular, so the appropriate verb form is "frustrates." The noun nearer the verb ("themes") is plural, but that is not the subject of the sentence. It is the object of a prepositional phrase.

A pronoun must agree with its antecedent, just as a verb must agree with its subject. If the word to which the pronoun refers is singular, the pronoun must be singular. Otherwise, both are plural.

Wrong: A phenomenologist will apply their philosophical method to a wide range of everyday experiences.

Right: Phenomenologists will apply their philosophical method to a wide range of everyday experiences.

In the first of the two preceding sentences, the plural pronoun "their" is paired with a singular subject. This problem was solved by making the subject plural. Solutions will vary from sentence to sentence.

A pronoun must have an explicit antecedent to which it refers. If the pronoun is the subject of a sentence, its antecedent should have appeared nearby in a previous sentence. If the antecedent precedes its pronoun by several sentences, the reader may lose track. Sometimes authors provide no antecedent at all. This is unacceptable. An author who has been writing about rationalism may use the word "they" to refer to rationalists, although the word "rationalists" has not been used. This is grammatically awkward and incorrect. The passage must be rewritten.

Case

A pronoun's case is the form it takes to display its role in the sentence as a subject, object, or possessor. Subjects take the subjective or nominative case (e.g., I, we, he, she, they, who). Objects of a verb or preposition take the objective case (e.g., me, us, him, her, them, whom). The possessive case shows ownership (e.g., my, our, his, her, their, whose).

Consider the following examples:

Wrong: Kierkegaard and me would not disagree that the ethical level of being is more advanced than the aesthetic.

Right: Kierkegaard and I would not disagree that the ethical level of being is more advanced than the aesthetic.

Wrong: John Wisdom and her are the only philosophers to approach language in that way.

Right: John Wisdom and she are the only philosophers to approach language in that way.

Wrong: The tutor sharply criticized Devon and I.

Right: The tutor sharply criticized Devon and me.

Wrong: Strawson is a better writer than him.

Right: Strawson is a better writer than he.

For the Kierkegaard examples, confirm the correct usage by mentally leaving out the first two words of each of the two sentences. Leave out the words "Kierkegaard and." You wouldn't begin a sentence by writing "Me would not disagree." You would begin with "I would not disagree." In compound subjects and objects, you can test your usage by keeping the pronoun and leaving out the other item. The correct pronoun is then usually obvious. The John Wisdom examples can be tested in the same way, although you have to change the plural verb to a singular one. You would not begin a sentence by writing "Her is the only philosopher." You would begin with "She is the only philosopher." Again, in the next set of examples, the same test can be applied. Would you write or say "The tutor sharply criticized I," or would you use the word "me"? The correctness of the second version becomes clear. Finally, the Strawson examples can be understood if you realize that an unstated "is" follows the last word of the sentence. We wouldn't say "than him is." We would say "than he is."

Misplaced Sentence Parts

Words or phrases are sometimes inserted in sentences at places where they simply do not fit. The results are awkward sentence structures and unnecessary sacrifice of a comfortable flow of wording for the reader. The bottom line is that the writing becomes less clear.

In some cases, entire phrases are misplaced. Consider this sentence:

> J. L. Austin examines the concept of responsibility in his essay, "A Plea for Excuses," which is very important in moral philosophy.

The author of this sentence meant that the concept of responsibility is very important in moral philosophy. However, the modifying phrase "which is very important in moral philosophy" was placed immediately after the title of the essay. This placement gives many readers the impression that the essay is very important in moral philosophy. Other readers may discern the ambiguity and be uncertain about the author's intention. The author would have avoided confusion by writing:

> J. L. Austin examines the concept of responsibility, which is very important in moral philosophy, in his essay, "A Plea for Excuses."

The rewording moves the dangling modifier (the "which is" phrase) so it is beside the word it modifies. This is a common solution for a common problem.

In other cases, moving a single word can make a big difference in the message that you convey. Notice what happens when the word *only* is placed differently in otherwise identical sentences. Although the word "fits" in each case, the meaning changes completely.

Professor Wu claimed that Socrates only wrote poetry.

Meaning: She claimed that Socrates wrote nothing besides poetry.

Professor Wu claimed that only Socrates wrote poetry.

Meaning: She claimed that no one else wrote poetry!

Professor Wu claimed only that Socrates wrote poetry.

Meaning: She claimed nothing else.

Only Professor Wu claimed that Socrates wrote poetry.

Meaning: No one else claimed it.

Missing Referents

The referent of a pronoun (the noun to which the pronoun refers) should be stated explicitly. The referent should occur in the same sentence or in one of the immediately preceding sentences. (The reader should not have to search back through what has already been read in order to find the noun.) The pronoun and its referent should agree in number. That is, they should both be singular or they should both be plural.

Read and compare these passages:

Wrong: Radical empiricism was doomed to failure. They were defending a thesis that was ultimately inconsistent.

Right: Advocates of radical empiricism were doomed to failure. They were defending a thesis that was ultimately inconsistent.

In the first passage, the pronoun "they" has no noun referent. Although the reader can probably figure out what the writer means, this kind of imprecise writing should be avoided. In the second passage, that same plural personal pronoun refers back to "advocates." Here the writer has been precise and eliminated the grammatical fuzziness.

Now consider this variation on the problem of a missing referent:

Wrong: In Baier's article, "Secular Faith," she discusses the importance of faith in the eventual attainment of a just society.

Right: In her article, "Secular Faith," Baier discusses the importance of faith in the eventual attainment of a just society.

The pronoun "she" is the subject of the first sentence. It occurs in the main clause, and "Baier," which occurs only in the prepositional phrase, is not a proper referent. In the second version, "Baier" is the subject, and may serve as a referent for pronouns in subsequent sentences.

Parallelism

Words, phrases, or sentences presented in series should be in parallel form. That is, multiple items presented as if they are on one level should share the same grammatical structure. In the following example the first sentence does not display parallel construction. The second sentence corrects the error.

Wrong: Wittgenstein wrote *Tractatus Logico-Philosophicus*, was the author of *Philosophical Investigations*, writing also "A Lecture on Ethics."

Right: Wittgenstein wrote *Tractatus Logico-Philosophicus, Philosophical Investigations*, and "A Lecture on Ethics."

Here the problem of having unparallel items in a series is solved by using one introductory verb and linking the items with commas. Sometimes different verbs must be used with various items in the series. An example follows.

Wrong: The pre-Socratic philosophers of ancient Greece wondered at the complexity of the world, had looked for a principle of unity in all the diversity, and claiming a principle of permanence in a sea of change.

Right: The pre-Socratic philosophers of ancient Greece wondered at the complexity of the world, looked for a principle of unity in all the diversity, and claimed a principle of permanence in a sea of change.

In this case, a different verb is part of each item in the series. In the corrected version, each verb has the same form. Here it is the preterit tense.

Lists sometimes display unparallel structure. Consider two versions of the same list:

Wrong: What do philosophers do? Their activities are diverse. Philosophers may be found doing the following sorts of things:

a. writing papers for publication in professional journals
b. teaching college classes
c. internships and residencies in prisons, schools, and even art museums
d. they are on ethics committees in hospitals
e. writing books for scholars
f. books for the public are sometimes written by philosophers
g. consulting for business and industry
h. serving on government task forces and committees.

Right: What do philosophers do? Their activities are diverse. Philosophers may be found doing the following sorts of things:

a. writing papers for publication in professional journals
b. teaching college classes
c. serving internships and residencies in prisons, schools, and even art museums
d. serving on ethics committees in hospitals
e. writing books for scholars
f. writing books for the public
g. consulting for business and industry
h. serving on government task forces and committees.

In the corrected version, parallel structure has been achieved by rewriting several of the items. An appropriate form for the items can be determined by reviewing the wording of the introductory passage. Here gerunds serve the purpose well. Often, the initial items in a series will take an appropriate form. Then you will forget how the introductory passage was worded and start creating various forms for later items. If you make this mistake, you should at least notice it when it is time to revise and edit the draft.

PUNCTUATION

Professors also expect correct punctuation. All punctuation marks have been misused at one time or another. Some kinds of misuse are common. The most common ones are noted here.

A **comma** should not be used to separate two complete thoughts—that is, two independent clauses. The result is one form of a "run-on" sentence, which is sometimes called a "comma splice."

> ***Wrong:*** Quine and Ullian wrote *The Web of Belief*, it has an especially well-written chapter on hypotheses.
>
> ***Right:*** Quine and Ullian wrote *The Web of Belief*. It has an especially well-written chapter on hypotheses.
>
> ***Also right:*** Quine and Ullian's *The Web of Belief* has an especially well-written chapter on hypotheses.

The comma does not provide a sufficiently strong separation between the two independent clauses in the original example. Each is capable of standing alone. The first solution is acceptable, but the second solution flows better and is more concise. Another misuse of the comma is its placement within a main clause where it is unnecessary.

> ***Wrong:*** William James's books are read, in both philosophy and psychology classes.
>
> ***Right:*** William James's books are read in both philosophy and psychology classes.

There is no need to set off the prepositional phrase with a comma. Short sentences like these seldom require a comma, except after an introductory word like "however" or "instead." The most basic of the several rules on avoiding incorrect comma placement is: Do not use a comma to separate the subject from its verb, the verb from its object, or an adjective from its noun.

Colons and **semicolons** are frequently misused and sometimes one is incorrectly used in place of the other. A colon (:) follows an introductory phrase that directs attention to what follows (after the colon). The writer should be wary of overuse of this symbol. A semicolon (;) separates two main clauses that could stand alone as sentences. The semicolon is used instead of a period to show a special relation between those two statements. Each illuminates the other. Semicolons have an additional use. They may be used to separate items in a series when a comma does not provide a sufficiently strong break because the items in the series are long or because they contain commas within themselves.

> ***Wrong:*** The continental rationalists of the seventeenth century believed that humans will avoid error if they initiate a line of reasoning with clear and distinct ideas; and deduce their logical implications.
>
> ***Right:*** The continental rationalists of the seventeenth century believed that humans will avoid error if they initiate a line of reasoning with clear and distinct ideas and deduce their logical implications.
>
> ***Also right:*** The continental rationalists of the seventeenth century believed that humans will avoid error if they initiate a line of reasoning with clear and distinct ideas and deduce their logical implications; they imagined that the patterns of the mind and the patterns of nature reflected one another.

The most common error involving semicolons is incorrect placement between two unequal parts of a sentence, when one is a main clause that can stand alone as a sentence, but the other is not. This error is illustrated in the first of the three preceding examples (the one labeled ***Wrong***). What follows the semicolon in that sentence cannot stand independently as a sentence. "And deduce their logical implications" is not a complete thought with subject and main verb. In the correction below that example, the semicolon is omitted. Below that, another example displays the correct use of a semicolon. Two main clauses that express related thoughts are joined by the semicolon.

An **apostrophe** shows possession or a contraction of two words. To show possession in the singular, you generally place an apostrophe at the end of the word and add *s*. To show possession in the plural, you generally place an apostrophe after the plural form of the noun, and you sometimes add *s* to that. The phrase "the empiricist's assumptions" refers to assumptions of one empiricist (who perhaps represents others). The phrase "the empiricists' assumptions" refers to assumptions of more than one empiricist (and possibly all empiricists). When an apostrophe is used to signal the contraction of two words into one, the apostrophe is placed where a letter has been omitted. We write "doesn't" rather than "doe'snt" because the *o* from the word *not* is omitted. Note an interesting case: *it's* is a contraction of *it is* (with the apostrophe marking the deleted *i*), leaving the possessive *its* to be spelled without an apostrophe, even though possession is also usually indicated with an apostrophe.

Finally, consider **quotation marks**. When you quote a passage word for word, use quotation marks before and after the borrowed words. However, when you write to convey the general sense of what was written or said, do not use quotation marks.

> ***Wrong:*** Karl Jaspers wrote that "we do not understand our own society because of its complexity and commotion." [The words in quotes are not Jaspers's own words.]

Right: Karl Jaspers wrote that we do not understand our own society because of its complexity and commotion. [The words that describe his comments are not Jaspers's own words.]

Also right: Karl Jaspers wrote, "Owing to the turmoil of modern life, what is really happening eludes our comprehension." [The words are the author's own or an English translation of them.]

In the first example, a reader might suspect the incorrect use of quotation marks because of the word *that.* However, if that word had not been included, the reader would be even more likely to believe that you were reporting an exact quote.

Sometimes you may want to leave out some words within a quoted passage. This is permissible if you don't misrepresent the original meaning and if you use an **ellipsis** of three spaced periods to indicate where the words were omitted. For example, you might want to quote part of the first sentence in the second paragraph of John Stuart Mill's *On Liberty.* Consider the whole sentence: "The struggle between liberty and authority is the most conspicuous feature in the portions of history with which we are earliest familiar, particularly in that of Greece, Rome, and England." If this quotation appears after the introduction of the topic of a conflict between liberty and authority, the writer may choose to delete the words "between liberty and authority" for more fluent reading. This is acceptable, but the deletion must be reported to the reader. The result should look like this: "The struggle . . . is the most conspicuous feature in the portions of history with which we are earliest familiar, particularly in that of Greece, Rome, and England."

GENDER

Some previously accepted uses of language should be avoided because of the gender inequities they can suggest. Use of the masculine pronoun in reference to groups that include males and females, for example, is no longer appropriate.

Wrong: A utilitarian has to be able to anticipate the actions of people he has never met in order to draw conclusions about the morally right course of action.

Also wrong: A utilitarian has to be able to anticipate the actions of people they have never met in order to draw conclusions about the morally right course of action.

Right: A utilitarian has to be able to anticipate the actions of people he or she has never met in order to draw conclusions about the morally right course of action.

Also right: Utilitarians have to be able to anticipate the actions of people they have never met in order to draw conclusions about the morally right course of action.

The first example displays the use of a masculine pronoun, *he*, to refer to male and female utilitarians. Avoid this old usage. A common attempt to resolve this difficulty is displayed in the second example. This approach to the problem is not acceptable, because we now have a plural pronoun, *they*, referring to a subject that is grammatically singular (although it is meant to refer to all utilitarians). The third example is grammatically correct, but the "he or she" phrase can be awkward, especially when it recurs frequently. The best solution is shown in the last example. The plural subject is referred to by a plural pronoun. This kind of solution is not always the best one. Solutions vary from case to case. Sometimes creative rewording of the sentence avoids the difficulty.

Replace the generic *man* with *humanity*. Pronoun references to the term are plural, so you could refer back to it with *they* instead of *his*. Also, replace *mankind* with *humankind*.

Finally, some philosophical issues are related to religious topics. Consider the question of gender identity before choosing a pronoun to refer to a divine being.

SCHOLARLY TERMS AND ABBREVIATIONS

You should recognize the most common scholarly terms and abbreviations so you understand what you read in academic journals and scholarly books. You will also benefit by being able to use these in your own academic writing when it is appropriate. Here is a sampling of terms and abbreviations (many of which are from Latin), along with a short definition of each, and an example of its correct usage. A few of these are more common in philosophy than in other disciplines, but all are at least sometimes found elsewhere.

Terms

a fortiori all the more. Such a being would not be conscious or sentient. *A fortiori,* it follows that such a being would not be self-aware.

ergo therefore. The argument from design fails to establish divine omnipotence, omniscience, or benevolence, *ergo* it is insufficient as a basis for belief in the Christian God.

necessary cause that without which the result or effect could not occur. Believing that the universe could not exist without divine foundations, Villard claimed that God was a necessary cause of our existence.

non sequitur doesn't follow; reasoning in which the evidence is irrelevant (or nearly so) to the conclusion. Leoni had nothing but a *non sequitur* to offer in support of the conclusion that Plato's claims about anamnesis were literally true.

pace peace; not meaning to offend, with apologies for differing. There is no doubt, *pace* Descartes, that animals are sentient beings.

passim throughout, in various parts (or *et passim*—"and throughout"). Gulley (1968: 22ff.) and Irwin (1977a: 36–38 *et passim*) have argued this before me.

posit to state as an accepted assumption. The professor is willing to posit, for the sake of conversation, the reality of mystical experience.

qua as, in the role of. She is considering the human being *qua* decision maker.

reductio ad absurdum an attack on a view by demonstrating its opposite to be impossible or foolish (also known as a "reductio"). The only way he could criticize the basic premise was by a *reductio ad absurdum*.

sine qua non that without which. The capacity for language is a *sine qua non* for higher intelligence.

sophistic subtle but misleading reasoning. A sophistic approach enabled the author to convince many readers to accept his faulty conclusions.

sufficient cause that which is itself enough to ensure a certain result or effect. The utopian claimed that equitable social institutions were a sufficient cause for social harmony.

sui generis one of a kind, unique. Are all the attributes of God *sui generis,* or are they comparable in some way to what we encounter in the world?

Abbreviations

cf. compare. On this point about Greek myth, cf. Pater (1908).

e.g. *exempli gratia,* for example. The titles of Austin's essays (e.g., "Three Ways of Spilling Ink" and "How to Talk—Some Simple Ways") may strike us as peculiar.

ff. and the following pages. For Wittgenstein's own explanation of the concept of "language games," see *The Blue Book,* p. 17ff.

ibid. *ibidem,* in the same place (as the preceding reference). [Commonly used in footnote references.]

i.e. *id est,* that is (to say). She is a philosopher of the best kind (i.e., a thinker who is both creative and rigorous, and who is not given to selecting her conclusions before examining the evidence).

op. cit. *opere citato,* in the work cited (previously). [Commonly used in footnote references.]

sic in this way. [Set off with brackets or parentheses, and used to indicate that a quoted passage containing an error or peculiarity is reproduced to reflect the original.] He had written that "this is a characteristically mail [*sic*] approach to ethical problem solving."

viz. namely. Kant analyzed aesthetics in what is known as his "third critique," *viz.,* his *Critique of Judgment.*

SPELLING

Spelling should be correct on all writing assignments that are prepared out of the classroom. Computer spellcheckers are helpful but not foolproof. Moreover, the responsibility for correct spelling is yours, whether or not you have employed spellcheckers and proofreaders.

Commonly Misspelled Words in Philosophy

Any list of commonly misspelled words for the English language is either very lengthy or highly selective. Let's narrow the scope. A list of commonly misspelled words in philosophy follows. Some readers will recognize a few that they regularly misspell.

aesthetic (in another correct spelling, the initial *a* is omitted)
analytic
anarchy
argument (the *u* is not followed by an *e*)
atheist
causal (not to be confused with the word *casual*)
coherence
conceive (follows the general guide rule, "*i* before *e*, except after *c*")
conscience
conscious
consciousness
deceive
deism
deontological
dialectical
dialogue
dualism
effect (often confused with *affect*)
empirical
empiricism
epiphenomenalism
except (not to be confused with *accept*)
existence (an *e* rather than an *a* follows the *t*)
existentialism
fallacy
medieval
necessary
ontological
perceive
phenomenology
philosophical
premise (*premiss* is an outdated spelling)

scholasticism
skepticism
solipsism
tautology
teleological
theism
theory
utilitarian

Conscience is an internal moral guide. *Conscious* is usually an adjective meaning "aware," but in Freudian psychology it has a noun form also. *Consciousness* is a noun related to the adjective *conscious*. *Effect* is usually a noun meaning something like "result." *Affect* is usually a verb meaning "to influence or have an effect on." (There are exceptions to this distinction between *effect* and *affect*. When we say, "He tried to effect [bring about] significant change in the political institutions," we are using *effect* as a verb. When we say, "He had an unusual affect [contrived demeanor or style] about him," we are using *affect* as a noun.)

Plurals of Philosophical Terms

Several words that are commonly used in philosophical discourse have plural forms about which many people are unclear. Here is a short list.

Singular	**Plural**
analysis	analyses
criterion	criteria
hypothesis	hypotheses
phenomenon	phenomena
schema	schemata
stratum	strata
thesis	theses

Analysis, hypothesis, schema, and *thesis* have plural forms with which many people are not familiar or comfortable. The other three words on the list—*criterion, phenomenon,* and *stratum*—demand attention because of the frequency with which people use the plural form when they intend a singular meaning. By grammatical definition, there is *never* one criteria, phenomena, or strata.

Capitalization

Capitalize the first letter of the first word in each sentence. Generally we do not capitalize the first word that follows a colon or semicolon unless it is a proper noun. Proper nouns—which name specific people (e.g., Georgios), places (e.g.,

Crete), things (e.g., the Colossus of Rhodes), or events (e.g., the Olympics)—must be capitalized, but not common nouns, which refer to items of a general kind (e.g., ball, spear, scroll, coin).

Proper nouns	**Common nouns**
Plotinus (is a specific example of a)	philosopher
Athens	city
Parthenon	temple
Panathenaia	festival

Do not capitalize simply for emphasis. For example, instead of writing, "Plato did Not claim that ideal human love is without a sexual aspect," emphasize the word *not* with italics—or just leave it without emphasis. (Some writers use italics too frequently.) Also, do not capitalize an entire word for emphasis (e.g., NOT).

Generally, we do not capitalize terms that name grand concepts in philosophy. We do not write *Absolute Values, Duties,* or *Responsibility.* These are common nouns. We simply write *absolute values, duties,* or *responsibility.*

6

Good Reasoning

In everyday life, people often use blustery overstatement to make their points. They deliver their conclusions without support, brandish sophistical reasoning, or resort to demeaning and intimidating language. They may dominate a conversation, and the very force of their presentation may substitute for impressive reasoning. Reread the section in Chapter 2 titled "Tone" if you need to be reminded that this kind of argumentation is quite different from what you should use in your philosophy papers.

Language must be precise. Appeal to reason rather than to rash and unreflective emotions. (This does not mean that a good paper will never call on the moral sensitivities of the reader.) Your conclusions should be supported by well-thought-out reasoning that would be compelling to, or at least worthy of consideration by, open-minded people who are neutral toward or skeptical about the view you offer. Be thorough as you detail your reasoning, and make explicit your assumptions even if you think the professor shares them with you (unless they are trivial or uncontentious).

Present your best reasoning. Use good logic. You can find entire books on how to reason well and avoid faulty inferences. For a strong focus on bias and fair reasoning, consider *Open Minds and Everyday Reasoning*, 2nd edition (Wadsworth, 2005) by Zachary Seech, which also has a chapter on writing thesis defense papers. For a strong focus on reasoning in the social and political arena, try *Logic and Contemporary Rhetoric*, 10th edition (Wadsworth, 2006) by Howard Kahane and Nancy Cavender. Each of these books explores kinds of evidence and basic rules of reasoning.

Sometimes you will be able to firmly establish claims that you make in your paper. At other times, you will have to settle for less. Be sure you don't claim that you have demonstrated more than you actually have. If one of the ways you support your claims turns out to be weak, delete it from the paper even though you may be fond of the point. Often, a paper writer, whether a student in college or a professor writing for other professors, will want to make a stronger claim than can be convincingly supported. The paper writer might be certain that the claim is true but unable to make a strong case for it in the paper. Self-discipline is required in these cases. What can you claim in your paper? Whatever you can support.

AN INTRODUCTORY EXAMPLE

A reasonable tone sets the stage for good reasoning but, of course, it does not by itself give anyone justification for believing you. It may give someone a reason for listening to you, but not a reason for believing you. You also need adequate evidence. For example, if you want to convince someone that a world government should replace the many different governments of present nations, some kinds of evidence will be more respectable than other kinds. The elimination of national rivalries that lead to wars and persecutions because of pettiness, vanity, and greed is an attractive advantage. Although others can respond with counterclaims—for example, that these problems would be regionalized rather than eliminated, or that disadvantages would outweigh these advantages—this point can still be part of a good argument if it is presented well. On the other hand, you don't want to say that a world government should be created because it is inconvenient to have different traffic rules in various nations. The difficulties inherent in disestablishing the current nations and creating and maintaining a new world government are certainly not worth the effort for mere convenience in a relatively insignificant matter. Even the weightier moral argument that laws on capital punishment should not vary, condemning some and sparing others arbitrarily, may seem insufficient to justify attempting such a formidable task as reworking the politics of the world.

Besides such general questions about how to support your thesis, you must also consider the specific logic of your reasoning. This chapter presents some patterns of reasoning that may help you make your case more clearly and convincingly.

MAKING A STRONG CASE FOR YOUR VIEW

You don't want your paper to be open to the criticism that it has unreliable premises, and you don't want it to be open to the criticism that it includes argumentation in which the premises are not sufficient to establish the conclusion. We should pause to think about what we mean by "establish the conclusion."

Sometimes the standard of making the premises prove the conclusion beyond any conceivable doubt is unrealistic. The evidence you offer for your thesis or for one of the subarguments supporting your thesis may establish its conclusion not with certainty, but with some degree of probability. This can be appropriate. If you are supporting the claim that "Outcome-based education, if implemented properly, would create an able citizenry for a democratic, high-technology state like the United States," we should expect you to *make a good case* that is worthy of consideration by reasonable people.

Be careful, however, to avoid overstating the certainty with which you have established the conclusion. Examine your opening and closing paragraphs to confirm that the thesis statements are in agreement, and that you have neither overplayed nor underplayed your logical hand. Comparing the wording of your thesis early and later in the paper can be important. Sometimes a paper writer will weaken the wording after finding that the case is not as strong as it had seemed. In other cases, fervor for the proposed point of view will build to the point at which the final version of the thesis is stated in a more extreme way.

Avoid using the phrase, "this leads to," to signal the move from premises to conclusion. First, it is too vague. A reader cannot know whether you intend to suggest that the conclusion has been proven beyond doubt. You should be explicit and precise as you lay out the logic of your argument. Use "therefore," "makes probable," or whatever is both appropriate and specific. Second, "leads to" is more commonly used in contexts other than reasoning: "love leads to marriage," "envy leads to strife," and "one thought leads to another (hardly related) thought." The banquet speaker says, "and that leads me to my final point" (which was not proven in any way by preceding ones). Again, the expression is vague.

Remember: If you find that you cannot adequately support a bold claim you have drafted into your paper, you have two alternatives. You can (1) claim to have established a probability or a strong possibility or an intriguing alternative, instead of claiming to have *proven* that the conclusion is true, or you can (2) weaken the claim by rewording it (e.g., by writing "most" rather than "all" or "better" rather than "best").

COUNTEREXAMPLES AND GENERALIZATIONS

Think carefully when you draft the word *all* into a paragraph, or when you use equivalent phrasing (e.g., *every, without exception*). One good counterexample disproves a universal claim. Thus, if you claim that "every human action is ultimately motivated by self-interest," a single example of an action that is *not* motivated by self-interest is sufficient to render your statement false. So it becomes important to avoid overstatement. If you can only defend the claim that something is true in "most" or "almost all" cases, resist the temptation to make the stronger universal (all) claim. If the several books on logic by Bertrand Russell that you have examined are all abstruse and technical, don't claim that "All of Bertrand Russell's writings are very technical." He also wrote popular articles on ethics and war. They are not technical; your claim would be false.

Notice the following problem in drafting broad statements. Sometimes your wording makes it clear that you intend a universal claim (e.g., "All of Plato's dialogues were written after the Peloponnesian Wars"). Sometimes your wording makes it clear that you intend only a generalization, a claim that is true in most but not all cases (e.g., "Most theories of truth from before the turn of the twentieth century were foundationalist"). In some other cases, the wording of the sentence does not clearly indicate whether a universal claim or a generalization was intended. For example, you may write, "Existentialists accept Sartre's view that 'existence precedes essence.'" The sentence may have been written like this with the intention of identifying a characteristic of every single existentialist.

However, the sentence may have been written like this with the intention of characterizing existentialists generally, and allowing for exceptions. Such imprecise wording should be avoided, unless the larger context (the other sentences in the paragraph or the thesis itself) clarifies your intention.

TWO KINDS OF MISDIRECTION

For some writers, *staying on track* is a challenge. They follow impulses as they write, forgetting the pattern of reasoning they had planned to present or becoming sloppy about the connections between their ideas. Guard against such undisciplined writing. Two problems that arise from a careless flow of ideas are straw men and tangents. Each is one way of "missing the point" as you write.

You set up a **straw man** whenever you attack a misrepresentation of someone's position or argument. For example, a straw man or counterfeit stand is attacked when a person who advocates the regulation of handguns is criticized as if she had proposed banning all handguns—a more radical (and different!) proposal. Straw men that are easier to attack than the actual position or argument are sometimes set up on purpose to make a weak case appear stronger. Often, however, they simply result from inattention or inadequate inquiry into that person's ideas.

A **tangent** is a side topic that, although related to the topic under discussion, is carried in directions that are not relevant to that discussion topic. When you are writing a paper, be wary of those aspects of the topic that you want to include (for whatever reason) but which have no proper place in the paper. In some kinds of writing, it's hard to tell when you're going off on a tangent, writing about something related to the main topic but not closely enough related to be included. In a thesis defense paper, there is a simple rule for what to include: *If it's good evidence for your conclusion or for one of the main points that you are using to support your conclusion, then include it in your paper. If it's related to your topic and interesting but doesn't provide more reason for believing the conclusion, then leave it out.*

FALLACIES

Writers commit fallacies when they use certain unreliable patterns of reasoning to argue for their conclusions. The names and descriptions of some of the logical fallacies that paper writers commonly commit follow.

A **false dilemma** is created when the author presents two alternatives as if they are the only ones possible, when in fact a third alternative exists. The reasoning offered by the creator of the false dilemma is this: If one of these alternatives is not true, then the other has to be true. But the simple either/or statement masks other possibilities. For example, an author carried away by blinding fervor for the thesis that capital punishment should be employed actively in all states of the union might proclaim that "we must universally adopt capital punishment unless we want crime running rampant and unchecked in every street." Is it true that without capital punishment, law and order will not be enforced anywhere in the nation? An inclination toward overstatement has set up what seems to be a false dilemma. Certainly, the author must modify the wording or argue specifically that the dilemma is not false and that this is the only possible alternative to the practice of capital punishment.

Extremism had a role in the preceding false dilemma. Avoid adopting such extreme points of view that you can defend only by closing your mind, overstating the case for your position, and unfairly attacking opposing positions and arguments.

The **fallacy of common belief** is committed when the author supports a claim that is not self-evidently true by observing that many people believe it to be true. False beliefs about the nature of the world, the human psyche, and certain races of people were at one time widespread. That did not make them true. Sometimes the grand claim that "everybody knows" is the disarming preface to such a claim. This fallacy would be committed if, for example, the writer (1) claims that men are generally better at spatial orientation tasks than women, or that women are generally better at verbal skills than men, then (2) supports the claim by writing that this must be true because the belief is so common or the "fact" is so well-known.

The **fallacy of two wrongs make a right** is committed when an action is justified only by identifying another, usually similar, action that someone else has taken. Clearly, as our parents told us years ago, one wrong doesn't justify a second one. You are not blameless for doing something shameful just because someone else did it first. Nevertheless, in politics and on various social topics, adults continue to commit this childhood fallacy. In your paper, don't argue that one act is defensible on the grounds that some others have acted similarly. This fallacy would be committed if, for example, the writer attempted a moral justification of American violation of some individuals' civil rights simply by observing that rival nations have committed acts that were in principle the same.

The **fallacy of slippery slope** is committed when the writer objects to an action or a social practice with the *unsubstantiated* charge that it will, with a "domino effect," lead to a series of similar but increasingly objectionable results, and ultimately to a dire or catastrophic end result. For example, someone might oppose teaching about the beliefs of the major religions in a public school curriculum by asserting that "the next thing" that will happen is that eventually some religions will be presented in a more favorable light than others, and "that will lead to" the explicit endorsement of some religions and the denigration of others, and that religion will "inevitably," then, become part of English, science, and even mathematics classes, and that this will spread beyond the public schools to other social institutions, and that ultimately the American principle of separation between church and state will be annihilated. To avoid the fallacy of slippery slope when you claim such a progression, you must establish the inevitability of each step in the progression or refrain from claiming inevitability.

In the **fallacy of contrary-to-fact hypothesis**, someone makes unknowable claims about what would have resulted if some event in the past had been different. For example, unqualified statements about how John F. Kennedy's presidency would have been viewed by future Americans if he had not been assassinated are statements that should be challenged. The same is true of claims about the results of the 1990 war in the Persian Gulf had anti-Iraqi forces moved on to Baghdad or had they remained as a stronger presence in the area. Speculation about such things is certainly understandable, and reasons can be given for particular conclusions. However, when arguing in a thesis defense paper, do not state *with an unreasonable degree of certainty* the results of events that might have occurred but did not.

The **fallacy of questionable cause** is committed when, on insufficient evidence, we identify a cause for something that happened or a fact that is true. Next to the false dilemma, this is probably the most common fallacy. We name one thing as the cause of another when there may have been other causes; we simply overlook the other possibilities. Why did the recent school shootings occur? What caused the decline in college entrance test scores over the past decades? Very often, the problem is not just that we latch onto the wrong cause. It's that we name as the sole cause something that is one of several contributing causes. In either of these versions, you have the ever-popular fallacy of questionable cause. In a rush to write a dynamic paper, don't fall prey to this kind of misassessment or oversimplification. If what you identify as a causal agent is a probable cause, and if you can make a good case for that, don't call it the certain cause. If what you identify is a contributing cause, don't brand it as the lone cause, even if the exact mix of contributing causes eludes you. Claim only as much as you can credibly defend.

TWO SPECIAL KINDS OF EVIDENCE

This chapter will close with comments on two kinds of evidence that might not be used at all in your philosophy papers. Testimonial evidence is not a part of most philosophy papers because authority is not a primary tool in philosophical analysis. Analogical evidence, the other kind to be examined here, is difficult to develop and seldom conclusive. Still, they are appropriate in some cases, and you should hear some words of caution.

Testimonial Evidence

In a thesis defense paper, because you are showcasing your reasoning skills and boldly claiming the truth of your thesis, you must be careful not to accept blindly even the word of authorities, although the paper may make some reference to them and even somewhat rely on them. People who get nationwide attention are not necessarily genuine authorities. Jerry Springer talks about sex topics regularly on his television show, and he interviews people with many sorts of unusual experiences. Yet his testimony on sexual psychology or morality would be worthless in an academic paper. He is not an expert in the field and should not be cited as one. The famous "Dr. Ruth" is more credible because she has training in the area and focuses much more on factual physiological research. Nevertheless, for a good academic paper you need to use topflight sources. On sexual matters, Janet Hyde is an example of an authoritative source. She is a professor of psychology at the University of Wisconsin and director of the Women's Studies Research Center there. She is also a member of the board of directors of the National Council for Research on Women, editor of the *Psychology of Women Quarterly*, and a fellow of both the American Psychological Association and the Society for the Scientific Study of Sex. She has written a well-known textbook on human sexuality and has worked on several studies in developmental psychology.

The testimony of credible persons sometimes strengthens your argument, but you almost always need to say *why* the reader should especially consider that person's comments. Give credentials. These may include academic degrees and professional experience. Don't assume, however, that respectable credentials alone establish the fact that we should accept the testimony without question. You should know when experts disagree on an issue, so that one expert's assessment does not alone establish the point. You should also realize that credentials that impress people outside the field of expertise may be deceptive. The president of the American Society of Professional Psychologists will command less credibility if we know that he founded this tiny group and is its only officer. At the very least, we need more information about his credentials before judging the authority of this source.

On some issues, even expert opinion will not add much to your own reasoning. The thesis defense paper should involve your own thinking. It should not be a compilation of quotes. In fact, testimonial evidence will always be of secondary importance in a philosophy paper. In the paper, you are displaying your own reasoning on an issue, and the testimony of others, if it is relevant at all, will be used only to give credibility to premises that you intend to employ as you develop your own line of reasoning. You should not claim that your thesis is true simply because someone else said or wrote that it is.

Use similar caution in citing publications. An unattributed article on sexual behavior in *Reader's Digest* or another popular magazine may be better ignored than mentioned, even if it supports your thesis. Although we all know that the printed and published word is not always truthful, many authors are tempted to use weak sources when good ones are not available. Does inclusion of the reference strengthen or weaken your paper? You have to use judgment. It varies with the topic, the source, and your line of argument. Popular magazines with light reading fare such as *Cosmopolitan* and *People* seldom, if ever, provide anything to strengthen an argument in a philosophy paper, and the sensationalizing tabloid newspapers are never respectable sources of evidence. Some other popular magazines, such as *The Atlantic Monthly, Harper's,* and *The New Yorker,* routinely publish articles with more analytical sophistication and depth. Still, you must consider each article on the basis of the author's credentials and the character of the written material.

Finally, avoid extensive quotes, and always give your own comment on the quote or reported view. Don't just report what the authority claims; after giving the quote, say why the reader should take it seriously and how it is related to your ideas. Remember that the thinking you showcase in your paper should be primarily your own.

Analogical Evidence

We use **analogies** to make points or illustrate ideas when we speak and when we write. In an analogy, we attempt to clarify one thing by comparing it with another that is similar in some way. Often the things compared are very different; they may be similar in only one respect.

In a simile, the wording includes an explicit expression of comparison. "His unusual cough was *like* the rattle of a loose ball bearing." In a metaphor, no explicit expression of comparison is used. "Housing developments of that sort are anthills." Similes and metaphors are simple kinds of analogies, but in argumentation we often reserve the term *analogy* for more complicated comparisons from which an insight or conclusion is to be drawn.

Analogies have been employed for ages. Plato, in Book V of his famous *Republic*, creates dialogue in which Socrates answers the question of whether women as well as men should hold the highest offices in an ideal political community. His response is the question: Would a bald man or a long-haired man be a better shoemaker? Obviously, hair distribution is a characteristic irrelevant to the cobbler's skill. Socrates suggests by analogy that gender is a characteristic irrelevant to skills of political leadership. Plato's *Republic* is full of argumentative analogies.

Analogies provide interest and rhetorical color to a line of reasoning. However, you must be cautious when you create your own analogy or evaluate someone else's. The logical power of an analogy is often overestimated. Usually, an analogy will help a person understand a relation and see new connections between things, but seldom does it provide hard proof of a conclusion or thesis for a person who ardently resists that view. Analogies are especially useful for articulating a new perspective that has just been supported with empirical evidence, because they often illustrate rather than establish points of view.

7

Internet and Other Research Sources

Many topics for philosophy papers require research. This chapter focuses on the activity of research. First, philosophical research through the Internet is explored with a look at the basics, and an introduction to specific websites for philosophical research. Second, philosophical journals, online and in print, are introduced. Finally, the roles of an academic library are discussed. See Chapter 8 for a description of the customary ways to acknowledge research sources.

THE INTERNET

Student research characteristically starts with the Internet. We are accustomed to reaching toward our keyboard when we have everyday research tasks. That's where we look for answers to questions like "What are the movie times at the theater tonight?," or "How many countries are there in Africa?," or "What are the risk factors for diabetes?" This is also where students most often initially inquire into a research topic for a paper to be written for an academic class.

Articles about research topics, or authors and their works, are available at the touch of several keys. Both information and analysis of issues can be found through topical searches. Through the Internet, we can identify books to be bought or borrowed. Often, the entire text of a classic philosophical book is available on our computer screens through the Internet. Various databases bring together extensive and varied sources on a single topic.

For both the student and the professor, research is frequently conducted in this electronic world. In earlier decades, it took a researcher years of experience in a specialty area to know which sources—authors, books, reference volumes—were available for a particular research task. It took a Ph.D. with years of experience and access to special collections in far-off libraries to even find some of the materials. Now an introductory student types in a word or phrase, and an electronic search instantly yields a list of sources on the topic. Although the expertise and experience are still invaluable, today's novice researcher has a powerful advantage over novice researchers of preceding generations.

What You Can Find on the Internet

You can read about every major philosopher on the Internet. You can learn about ancient Greek philosophers, like Socrates, Plato, and Aristotle. You can learn about Roman philosophers, such as the famous stoic emperor Marcus Aurelius. You can learn about medieval philosophers, such as Saint Thomas Aquinas. There will also be articles on Renaissance thinkers, as well as every noted philosopher through the twentieth and into the twenty-first century. Some of the Internet articles are biographies; some are summaries and analyses of classic writings. Of these Internet articles, some are written by professors and professional scholars, and some are written by novices. *For your academic research, make sure you know who has authored the articles you use.* For specific cautions on this important matter, read "How to Evaluate It" later in this chapter.

General philosophical topics can be researched in Internet territory as well. You can look up "Business ethics" or "Existentialism" or "Logical Positivism" and find a list of online resources. Here again, be careful to rely on well-authored material. You should know the credentials of whoever has written the Internet article. Professional philosophical journals are periodical publications in which credentialed philosophers articulate their views, interpret and critique the views of both historical and contemporary philosophers, and review recently authored books in philosophy. Many of these journals are now accessible online, sometimes through individual or library subscription, and sometimes without restriction.

Entire books in philosophy are also available on the Internet. The whole of Plato's *Republic*, Descartes's *Meditations*, and scores of other works in philosophy can be read on your computer monitor or copied with your printer. See "Where to Find Books Online" in this chapter.

Philosophy papers sometimes require research from areas outside of philosophy itself. For example, a paper for an ethics class might be on the topic of capital punishment. Evidence offered in support of the paper's thesis might include information on the cost of housing convicts in prison and the cost of execution. The thesis might require evidence about whether capital punishment is a significant deterrent to particular crimes. This kind of information comes from sources outside philosophy, and much of this can be found through the Internet. Here is another example. The philosophical problem of the relation between mind and body now is addressed with information from the "cognitive scientists" in the disciplines of chemistry, neurology, linguistics, and psychology. A philosophy paper on this topic would appropriately include information and analysis from these areas. Again, the Internet is a valuable resource. Some of the relevant research can be accessed directly through the Internet, and other resources (e.g., books, printed periodicals, and experts to consult) may be mentioned there for your further research.

How to Find It

Search engines are programs that enable you to look up websites. You type in a word or phrase, such as "empiricism" or "logical positivism," or a name, such as "Aristotle." Then you are presented with a list of sites that may be related to that topic.

The most popular and powerful general search engines are found at *google.com* and *yahoo.com*. These are quite "powerful" in that they yield long lists of sites. This is also their weakness. They give you long unedited lists that include many sites not relevant to your specific purpose. For example, when you type in "Pythagoras" in search of information on the ancient Greek philosopher who is often credited with discovering the "Pythagorean theorem" you learned in high school geometry, you may encounter a list of more than a million websites, and some will have nothing to do with philosophy. For example, some products and services have Pythagoras for a name. A computer consulting firm and a developer of websites are among the items that come up under the name Pythagoras, as well as a project to strengthen research teams at the Agricultural University of Athens. You may also encounter a website on Pythagoras Lodge #659, which is a fraternal fellowship in Houston, and a site peddling a CD-ROM ("In the distant future, the exploration vessel Spaceship Pythagoras is attacked . . ."). When you type in "Augustine" in search of information on the early Christian bishop who was an important philosopher, you may be presented with more than fifteen million (!) references, including the Augustine Golf Club, St. Augustine's Alligator Farm, and Bottomline Yacht and Boat Sales of St. Augustine, Florida. On both Google and Yahoo, you can select Advanced Search to focus your customized inquiry. Even though it is possible to narrow or "refine" your search, this process is often unsatisfactory.

Some other general search engines are Microsoft Live Search (*live.com*), *ask.com, search.aol.com, altavista.com, lycos.com*, and *search.netscape.com*. The search methods for the engines vary. Most engines now list sites with key words that appear in the text of that site. The word or phrase is found on particular sites by means of a robotic "crawler" that seeks out the terms you have typed in. A few still list at least partly according to "directories" that are categorized and overseen by human editors. Even the engines that are almost exclusively powered by crawlers will yield somewhat different lists.

Limited area search engines conduct searches that are specific to certain fields of inquiry. Noesis is a limited area search engine that searches for philosophy texts and sites. It is free and it is administered and edited by a team of respected academic philosophers. You can access it at *noesis.evansville.edu*. By clicking on "about" at the home page, you can view the academic credentials of Anthony Beavers, the editor of the site, as well as those of the associate editor, the editorial consultant, and the members of the advisory board. You can also read about the ways they edit the list of sites to be searched by this search engine.

Some websites for accessing philosophical research include among their various features certain custom search engines. For example, at EpistemeLinks (pronounced epi-stay-may links), you can search the combined entries of the Stanford Encyclopedia of Philosophy and the Internet Encyclopedia of

Quick Reference to Philosophy Websites

- American Philosophical Association resources, apa.udel.edu/apa/resources
- EpistemeLinks, epistemelinks.com
- Internet Encyclopedia of Philosophy, iep.utm.edu
- Noesis, noesis.evansville.edu
- Stanford Encyclopedia of Philosophy, plato.stanford.edu

Philosophy. These two online encyclopedias are free. They are well-edited and their articles are authored by credentialed academic philosophers. The Stanford Encyclopedia of Philosophy is located at *plato.stanford.edu*, and the Internet Encyclopedia of Philosophy is at *iep.utm.edu*. From each home page, you can access information on who the editors are and how the site is managed.

EpistemeLinks, which can be found at *epistemelinks.com*, is well-known among contemporary philosophers, and offers a variety of research services in philosophy. Besides the custom search engine to access and search the two online encyclopedias mentioned in the preceding paragraph, there is a search engine to access online texts ("e-texts") of many classic philosophical writings. At EpistemeLinks, you can also find thousands of links to: audio and visual resources, bibliographies, blogs, course materials, student aids to writing and studying, university philosophy departments, discussions, images, journals, quotations, software, philosophy timelines, and book locators. There is also a list of Latin phrases that are used in academic writing.

For more links of similar kinds, consult the official website of the American Philosophical Association's index of Web resources at *apa.udel.edu/apa/resources*. The lists here of "Guides to Philosophy" and "Directories" may be helpful. There are various other websites through which you can access research information in philosophy, and many of these reference others, through which you can find yet others. EpistemeLinks is a good place to start. For primary and secondary texts on the classics of the ancient world, not exclusively in philosophy, go to *perseus.tufts.edu*.

How to Evaluate It

The quality of Internet sites and the expertise of their authors vary from world-famous, top-notch reliability to extreme unreliability. Sometimes the unreliable sites are not easily distinguishable from the more reliable ones, except by an expert in the field. No credentials in philosophy are required for Internet publication on a philosophical topic.

If you purchase an academic or scholarly book published by a reputable publisher, you can expect that the seasoned caution of the publisher's subject-area editor and the criticism of the prepublication expert reviewers provide a likelihood that the book is at least generally reliable. These reviewers usually provide the editor with written assessments of a partial or complete draft of the book. With these reviews in hand, the editor decides whether to sign a contract for the book, and then (with copy or developmental editors) how to guide the author through revision of the work. Even with these safeguards, the reader has to exercise caution in accepting claims in the book.

On the Internet, anyone may "publish." Therefore, the researcher who seeks reliable information and analysis must be especially careful. Here are some suggestions:

1. Know about the author of the site. Many sites have a section in which you may read about the author's background. Here you might discover, for example, that the author has a Ph.D. in philosophy from a major university, has researched the special area this site focuses on, and has authored articles and/or books on the topic. Then, if you choose, you can investigate further by conducting a search based on the author's name, academic affiliation, and publications.
2. Use guides and directories that you know are managed by experts and/or based at reputable institutions. Noesis, the American Philosophical Association, and institutes or research centers at major universities are examples.
3. Remember that reliability is not an all-or-nothing matter. Just as you cannot be certain that every statement by a distinguished professor is true, or every book in an academic library is wholly reliable, you cannot be certain that there is no error on even the best internet sites. This issue is even subtler on philosophical topics in which information and analysis intertwine. There are gradations of reliability, and each source should be studied as a guide rather than as final authority.
4. Consult more than one source, as you should with printed research sources, to confirm claims or to encounter differing perspectives.

Many students start their research projects at *wikipedia.com*. Wikipedia is an online encyclopedia with articles that *anyone* may author or alter, although attentive editing by unpaid Wikipedia staff and by other contributors strengthen the articles and generally result in a useful starting point for learning about a new topic. Still, this is not a source to be cited as authoritative in an academic paper, whether in philosophy or any other discipline. Newer articles are less reliable than the older ones that have been through much review and editing. Even when information is correct, significant omissions are often problematic. A basic principle in the citation of authority is that you know whose words are being cited and you know the professional credentials of the writer. There are not many justified exceptions to this principle. Authors are not identified on Wikipedia, and articles may result from the combined contributions of more *and* less qualified contributors.

Many guides for the evaluation of scholarly sites are available on the Web. You can search through Google or Yahoo or any general search engine for "Evaluating Internet" and you will come up with many helpful sites. The University Libraries at Virginia Tech offer an online tutorial in which you actually review websites to apply various principles of evaluation. It's at *lib.vt.edu/help/instruct/evaluate/evaluating.html*. Their bibliography of other such sites may also be useful. It's at *lib.vt.edu/help/instruct/evaluate/evalbiblio.html*.

Where to Find Books Online

You can purchase books on the Internet through many vendors. Through the popular Amazon (*amazon.com*), Barnes and Noble (*barnesandnoble.com*), and Powell's (*powells.com*), you can order even many out-of-print books for mail delivery. However, some websites publish the full text of major works of historical significance. Some of these are philosophical classics. The digital library provided by the University of Pennsylvania at *digital.library.upenn.edu/books* is one good place to start. Another is Columbia University's digital text library at *ilt.columbia.edu/publications/digitext.html*, which is a source for the full text of works by Aristotle, Bentham, Berkeley, Descartes, Dewey, Emerson, Hegel, Hobbes, Hume, Kant, Leibniz, Locke, Machiavelli, Mill, Plato, Rousseau, Socrates, and Spinoza. A site specific to seventeenth- and eighteenth-century thinkers is *earlymoderntexts.com*, where you can find works by Bacon, Berkeley, Descartes, Edwards, Hobbes, Hume, Kant, Leibniz, Locke, Malebranche, Mill, Newton, Reid, and Spinoza. Dozens of other sites for full-text philosophical works can be accessed through the Hanover College's directory at *history.hanover.edu/etexts.html#general.*

You can also search and find websites that are dedicated specifically to the publication of the translated works of one philosopher, such as the seventeenth-century French philosopher Rene Descartes (*renedescartes.com*) or the nineteenth-century German philosopher Friedrich Nietzsche (*geocities.com/thenietzschechannel/ntexteng.htm*). Try typing "full text" and the name of the philosopher into your general search engine.

There are drawbacks to not having a physical copy of a book you are studying in detail. It is difficult to study large documents on a computer, especially when moving between various passages. With a printer, you can print out a hard copy of the work, but that can take a lot of time, paper, and ink. Also consider that many classic philosophical works were not originally written in English, and that some of these have been translated by various translators. For example, although it is easy to find versions of Plato's dialogues online, almost every one of these is translated by Benjamin Jowett in the nineteenth century. By contemporary standards, the writing is stilted, and much of the irony and humor does not come through well to modern ears. If you have questions about which translation to use, ask your professor.

JOURNALS, REFERENCE WORKS, AND LIBRARIES

Academic, public, and private libraries house books, periodicals (including scholarly journals), and research specialists that can be instrumental and sometimes essential to the success of your research project and the quality of your paper. In addition, through the scholarly subscriptions of your academic library, you may be able to access research sources that would otherwise be too expensive.

Let's start with journals. Scholarly journals in the various academic disciplines are periodicals to which scholars and libraries subscribe. In philosophy journals, most articles are written by professors. Occasionally, however, a published article is written by a scholar who is not affiliated with the faculty of an educational institution.

Besides articles (ranging in length from a few pages to thirty or forty pages), philosophical journals may publish less formal "discussions," responses to other articles, and reviews of new books in the field.

Because journal discourse is typically intended for other scholars in the field, it is sometimes difficult for students—including philosophy majors—to read. Technical language is often employed, and familiarity with previous work on the topic (in articles or books) may be assumed. The accessibility to undergraduates varies among journals and articles. Sometimes no special preparation at all is assumed.

The contents of a printed, non-electronic issue of a journal, with each article's title and author, are listed on the front cover, on the back cover, or on one of the opening pages. The institutional affiliation of the author is often indicated at the beginning or end of each article. Here is a partial list of well-known and topical journals in philosophy that publish most articles in English:

American Philosophical Quarterly
Analysis
Ancient Philosophy
The Australasian Journal of Philosophy
Behavior and Philosophy
Business Ethics Quarterly
Dialectica
Dialogue: Canadian Philosophical Review (English and French)
Economics and Philosophy
Environmental Ethics
Ethics
Film and Philosophy
Hypatia: A Journal of Feminist Philosophy
Inquiry
International Journal for Philosophy of Religion
International Philosophical Quarterly
Journal of Aesthetics and Art Criticism
Journal of Medicine and Philosophy
Journal of Philosophy
Journal of Social Philosophy
Journal of the Philosophy of Sport
Journal of Value Inquiry

Mind
Monist
Nous
Philosophical Psychology
Philosophical Quarterly
Philosophical Review
Philosophy
Philosophy and Phenomenological Research
Philosophy and Public Affairs
Philosophy East and West
Philosophy of Science
Ratio
Review of Metaphysics

This is just a sampling of the many journals in philosophy. Most publish a numbered issue twice, three times, or four times a year. Some journals are available only in paper form and are mailed to subscribing individuals and institutions like, perhaps, your academic library. Some are published in both paper and electronic form, or in some combination of the two. Some journals are exclusively electronic. The current and previous tables of contents for many of the journals are published online. For the website of a journal, type into the search field (a) the name of the journal and (b) the word "journal," if it is not included in that name (as in "Journal of . . ."). Sometimes it helps to also type in the word "philosophy."

To get a copy of an article, check to see if it is available without restriction (i.e., without cost) online. If it is not, check whether your library has a subscription to the journal, either in a paper version or electronically with online or CD access. If not, you can complete an Interlibrary Loan (ILL) request form, and your academic library will borrow the journal or acquire a photocopy of the journal article from another library. On this form, you would provide the journal name, the title and author of the article, the volume, and the issue name and number for the journal article. If possible, provide page numbers of the article also.

You can gain access to your library's subscription to journals (often through JSTOR or EBSCO databases) or to other special resources in philosophy at your academic library, and in many cases at home with your own computer, using either (a) a password provided to you at the library or (b) your student number. To find out how this works on your campus, go to your university library's website or telephone a reference librarian at the library.

One research database worth knowing about is *The Philosopher's Index*. The Philosophy Documentation Center (*pdcnet.org*) is a nonprofit organization that provides subscription access to a range of philosophical materials. Through their POIESIS database of philosophy journals, the full text of more than fifty journals can be viewed and searched for key words or combinations of words.

The hardcover volumes of the *Encyclopedia of Philosophy,* published in 1967 and supplemented in 1996, can still be found in innumerable academic, public, and private libraries. There is now a second edition (2005) that has been both updated and expanded. Donald M. Borchert is the editor of the newer edition.

In 1998, the ten-volume *Routledge Encyclopedia of Philosophy* (REP) was published. It has an online, slightly more extensive version, *Routledge Encyclopedia of Philosophy Online,* to which your library may have an institutional subscription. Here you can find entries on philosophical themes such as "Epistemology," "Science," "Language," and "Religion." You can find entries on world philosophies by region such as "African" and "Latin American." You can find entries on philosophic thought during certain periods such as "Ancient," "Renaissance," and "19th Century." You can also find entries on religious philosophies such as "Islamic" and "Hindu."

In your library's collection of shelved books, there will probably be many special reference volumes that provide an overview of philosophy in general, of a philosophical movement or thinker, or of philosophical terminology. Here is a sampling of this kind of resource:

Angeles, Peter A. *HarperCollins Dictionary of Philosophy.* 2nd ed. New York: HarperCollins, 1992.

Becker, Lawrence C., ed. *Encyclopedia of Ethics.* 2nd ed. New York: Routledge, 2001.

Blackburn, Simon. *The Oxford Dictionary of Philosophy.* Oxford: Oxford University Press, 1996.

Blackwell Philosopher Dictionaries. For example:

Inwood, Michael. *A Heidegger Dictionary.* Oxford: Blackwell, 1999.

Glock, Hans-Johann. *A Wittgenstein Dictionary.* Oxford: Blackwell, 1996.

Bunnin, Nicholas, and JiyuanYu. *Blackwell Dictionary of Western Philosophy.* Oxford: Blackwell, 2004.

Carr, Brian, ed. *Companion Encyclopedia of Asian Philosophy.* New York: Routledge, 1997.

Flew, Antony. *A Dictionary of Philosophy.* New York: Gramercy, 1999.

Kraut, Richard. *The Cambridge Companion to Plato.* Cambridge: Cambridge University Press, 1993.

Lacey, A. R. *A Dictionary of Philosophy.* 3rd ed. New York: Barnes & Noble, 1999.

Mautner, Thomas. *Penguin Dictionary of Philosophy.* New York: Penguin, 1998.

Peters, F. E. *Greek Philosophical Terms.* New York: New York University Press, 1991.

Post, Stephen Garrard, ed. *Encyclopedia of Bioethics.* 5 vols. New York: Macmillan, 2004.

Schuhmacher, Stephan, and Gert Woerner. *The Encyclopedia of Eastern Philosophy and Religion.* Boston: Shambhala, 1994.

Stewart, David, and Algis Mickunas. *Exploring Phenomenology: A Guide to the Field and Its Literature.* Athens: Ohio University Press, 1990.

Stockhammer, Morris, comp. *Kant Dictionary.* New York: Philosophical Library, 1972.

———. *Plato Dictionary.* New York: Philosophical Library, 1963.

Urmson, J. O. *The Greek Philosophical Vocabulary.* London: Duckworth, 2001.

———, and Jonathan Ree. *The Concise Encyclopedia of Western Philosophy and Philosophers.* London: Routledge, 1993.

Among the standard histories of Western philosophy are Will Durant's classic *The Story of Philosophy,* Frederick Copleston's detailed and respected *A History of Philosophy,* and Wallace I. Matson's well-written *A New History of Philosophy.* For a historical anthology that includes the last half of the twentieth century, there is *Philosophic Classics: Plato to Derrida,* by Forrest E. Baird and Walter Kaufmann. To locate these and other books on the shelves of your library, go to the electronic catalog of the library's holdings, usually accessible on specified computer terminals at the library, and identify the call number on the spine of the book. At your academic library, you can expect that the call numbers will be arranged according to the Library of Congress (LOC) classification system. Most works in philosophy will have a letter-number designation that begins with the letter B. With the complete call number of the book, you can identify the book's exact location on the shelves. For help in navigating the catalog or other resources of the library, ask a reference librarian or research librarian for help.

8

References to Other Sources

You must acknowledge all the sources you use in developing a paper. Mentioning the name of the author of the source or even giving the title of a book or article is not enough. The reader should be able to look up the acknowledged sources, recreating the original research process. It is your duty to give complete publication information. All this detailed information about sources can be included in the text of the paper itself. Among the disadvantages of this approach is the interruption of the flow of ideas that develop the themes of the paper. Scholars have developed the practice of listing sources at the end of a paper and identifying specific references throughout the paper. No single method of doing this has been accepted by all the world's scholars, but a few approaches have become professional standards. Some scholarly disciplines have their own formats.

Most college writing follows one of two basic systems. In one system, notes are placed at the bottom of the pages of the paper (footnotes) after having been signaled in the text by asterisks or superscript numbers. In the other system, parentheses in the text enclose a reference to an author from the list of works cited and designate the page numbers in the work. Each of these systems and the rules for arranging the information are explained in this chapter.

BIBLIOGRAPHY

A bibliography at the end of the paper lists the sources used in the development of the paper. From the ancient Greek, the word *bibliography* almost literally means "write down the books." In a modern bibliography, books are often the most numerous sources. However, you may also include articles, nonprint sources, and Internet sites.

Bibliographies may list not only works cited, but also works consulted though not referred to in the paper. When the bibliography lists only works that are actually cited, it is often titled "Works Cited."

Add the bibliography to the end of the paper. It should have a page number for each of its pages, continuing the pagination of the paper itself. If the closing paragraph of the paper ends on page 12, the bibliography should begin on page 13. Short papers often have a bibliography that consists of only one page.

The works should be listed alphabetically by the authors' last names. When no author is indicated for a work, use the title of the work and enter it alphabetically into the list that is otherwise ordered by author. When alphabetizing a title, ignore the opening word if it is a definite or indefinite article: *The, A,* or *An.* However, include that word as you write the title in the entry.

Listing Books

A bibliographic entry has three major elements: (1) author's name, (2) title of the work, and (3) publication information. Sometimes additional information is required. This depends on the type of publication, as you will discover in this chapter.

The kind of source being listed determines the form of the entry. Identifying books is somewhat different from identifying articles, other printed matter, nonprint material such as films and broadcasts, and Internet sources.

For references to books, the information is usually arranged in the following order, although not all of these elements are always applicable:

1. Author's name: Last name, comma, first name, period. (To include a second author, replace the period with a comma and then add the second author without reversing first and last names.)
2. Title: Full title italicized or underlined, period. If there is a subtitle, write main title, colon, subtitle. (If only one specialized part of the book has been used [e.g., a preface or an appendix], give that title, then a period, then the book title.)
3. Editor or translator's name: First name, then last name, preceded by *Ed.* or *Trans.* and followed by a period.
4. Edition: 2nd ed., 3rd ed., etc. (First editions do not require this entry.)
5. Volume number: *Vol. 2.* if only Volume 2 of a multivolume work was used; *5 vols.* if the work has five volumes and more than one was used.
6. Series name: for example, *Foundations of Philosophy Series.* For a titled series of books. (Most books are not part of a series.)
7. Publisher: City in which published (and the state, if there is any question about it), colon, publishing company, comma, year of publication (e.g., New York: Norton, 1993). (All this is available on the opening pages of the book. If more than one city is identified, use the first.)
8. Page numbers: Listing of a specialized part of the book (e.g., appendix, preface, article) if only that part was used. (This part of an entry is seldom necessary.)

The first line of each entry should be flush with the left margin. Any additional lines for that entry should be indented several spaces, with the result that the first line hangs out over the rest on the left side. Double-space all entries. Here are some sample bibliographic entries for books.

A Book by One Author

Ingram, David. *Critical Theory and Philosophy*. New York: Paragon, 1990.

Nussbaum, Martha C. *The Fragility of Goodness*. Cambridge: Cambridge University Press, 1986.

A Book with Coauthors

Brickhouse, Thomas C., and Nicholas D. Smith. *Socrates on Trial*. Princeton: Princeton University Press, 1990.

Smart, J. J. C., and Bernard Williams. *Utilitarianism: For and Against*. Cambridge: Cambridge University Press, 1973.

An Anthology of Collected Work

Kittay, Eva Feder, and Diana T. Meyers, eds. *Women and Moral Theory*. Savage, MD: Rowman & Littlefield, 1987.

McMullin, Ernan, ed. *The Concept of Matter in Greek and Medieval Philosophy*. Notre Dame: University of Notre Dame Press, 1963.

An Article in an Anthology

Lee, Edward N. "Reason and Rotation: Circular Movement as the Model of Mind (Nous) in the Later Plato." *Facets of Plato's Philosophy*. Ed. W. H. Werkmeister. Assen: Van Gorcum, 1976. 70–102.

Russell, Bertrand. "Logical Atomism." *Logical Positivism*. Ed. A. J. Ayer. New York: Free Press, 1959. 31–50.

A Book with an Author and an Editor

Hume, David. *An Inquiry Concerning Human Understanding*. Ed. Charles W. Hendel. Indianapolis: Bobbs-Merrill, 1955.

Mill, John Stuart. *The Subjection of Women*. Ed. Susan Moller Okin. Indianapolis: Hackett, 1988.

A Book with a Translator

Camus, Albert. *The Stranger*. Trans. Stuart Gilbert. New York: Vintage, 1946.

Kant, Immanuel. *Critique of Pure Reason*. Trans. Norman Kemp Smith. New York: St. Martin's, 1933.

A Multivolume Work

Guthrie, W. K. C. *The Earlier Presocratics and the Pythagoreans*. Cambridge: Cambridge University Press, 1962. Vol. 1 of *A History of Greek Philosophy*. 6 vols. 1962–1981.

Jaspers, Karl. *Philosophy*. Trans. E. B. Ashton. 3 vols. Chicago: University of Chicago Press, 1969–1971.

A Book in a Series

Walsh, James J., and Henry L. Shapiro, eds. *Aristotle's Ethics: Issues and Interpretations*. Wadsworth Studies in Philosophical Criticism. Ed. Alexander Sesonske. Belmont, CA: Wadsworth, 1967.

Wittgenstein, Ludwig. *Tractatus Logico-Philosophicus*. Trans. D. F. Pears and B. F. McGuinness. International Library of Philosophy and Scientific Method. New York: Routledge & Kegan Paul, 1960.

A Book in Another Language

Herodotus. *Herodoti Historiae* [*Herodotus's Histories*]. Carolus Hude, ed. 3rd ed. Oxford: Clarendon, 1927.

Unamuno, Miguel de. *El Espejo de la Muerte* [*The Mirror of Death*]. 7th ed. Colección Austral. Madrid: Espasa-Calpe, 1941.

An Introduction, Preface, Foreword, Afterword, or Appendix

Husserl, Edmund. Author's Preface to the English Edition. *Ideas: General Introduction to Pure Phenomenology*. By Husserl. Trans. W. R. Gibson. New York: Collier, 1962. 5–22.

Koestenbaum, Peter. Introductory essay. *The Paris Lectures*. By Edmund Husserl. The Hague: Martinus Nijhoff, 1970. ix–lxxvii.

An Article in a Reference Work

"Logos." *Greek Philosophical Terms: A Historical Lexicon*. F. E. Peters. New York: New York University Press, 1967.

Warnock, G. J. "Reason." *Encyclopedia of Philosophy*. 1967 ed.

Listing Articles in Periodicals

Periodicals are issued "periodically." They are publications that are published in issues that are brought out at regular intervals (e.g., weekly or monthly). Philosophy papers that focus on academic philosophical themes typically refer to more scholarly journals than other kinds of periodicals. These contain articles that are written by professional philosophers and directed to their colleagues. Philosophy papers on general themes such as practical ethics or public policy may have more magazines and newspapers as sources.

A bibliographic entry for a periodical has the same three major elements as an entry for a book: (1) author's name, (2) title of the work, and (3) publication information. In periodical citations, the information is usually arranged in the following order:

1. Author's name: Same form of entry as that for books.
2. Title: Enclosed within quotation marks. Period precedes closing quotation mark.
3. Name of periodical: Italicized or underlined.
4. Series, volume, and issue number: Only for journals, though most have no series number. (A special series is sometimes identified with a name instead of a number.)
5. Publication date and page numbers: For journals, year of publication in parentheses, colon, page numbers of article. For other periodicals, date without parentheses, edition (if any), colon, page numbers, period.

Here are some sample bibliographic entries for periodicals.

A Magazine Article

Church, George J. "Splinter, Splinter Little State." *Time* 6 July 1992: 36–39.

Kinoshita, June. "Dreams of a Rat." *Discover* July 1992: 34–41.

A Newspaper Article

Hoyle, Martin. "Dazzling Journey into Moral Maze." *Times* [London] 8 June 1992, arts: 2.

Ollman, Leah. "New Visions of Public Art in San Diego." *Los Angeles Times* 1 July 1992, San Diego edition: F1.

A Scholarly Journal

Journals have a volume number for a set of issues (called numbers). Volume 12 of a journal may be issued in four issues/numbers. The second issue of volume 12 is designated in the bibliographic entry like this: *12.1.* If each issue begins with page one, you must give volume and issue number. If the journal paginates continuously from one issue of a volume number to another (e.g., issue 2 may begin on page 165), you may omit the issue number and the month or season of publication.

Journals publish reviews of books in the field as well as original articles. *Rev. of* stands for "review of." Also note that the Gale entry that follows refers to a monograph series in which a single paper is published in each issue, so page numbers are unnecessary. Finally, when there are two or more consecutive entries for the same author, all entries subsequent to the first show________. where the name would otherwise be located (at the beginning of the entry). See the Vlastos entries in this list.

Bailin, Sharon. "Critical and Creative Thinking." *Informal Logic* 9 (1987): 23–30.

Flax, Neil M. Rev. of *Positions* by Jacques Derrida. *Philosophy and Literature* 5 (1981): 237–38.

Gale, Richard. "Negation and Non-Being." *American Philosophical Quarterly* monograph series 10 (1976).

Gracia, Jorge J. E. "Texts and Their Interpretation." *Review of Metaphysics* 43 (1990): 495–542.

Hayry, Matti, and Heta Hayry. "AIDS in a Small North European Country—A Study in Applied Ethics." *International Journal of Applied Philosophy* 3.3 (Spring 1987): 51–61.

Herman, Barbara. "Mutual Aid and Respect for Persons." *Ethics* 94 (1984): 577–602.

Ketchum, Sara Ann, and Christine Pierce. "Rights and Responsibilities." *Journal of Medicine and Philosophy* 6 (1981): 271–79.

Monserrate, Jaime E. Toro. "De Wittgenstein a la filosofía de la acción. " *Dialogos* 17.39 (Apr. 1982): 71–80.

Prasad, Rajendra. "The Concept of Moksa." *Philosophy and Phenomenological Research* 31 (1971): 381–93.

Stough, Charlotte L. "Forms and Explanation in the 'Phaedo.'" *Phronesis* 21.1 (1976): 1–30.

Vlastos, Gregory. "Is the 'Socratic Fallacy' Socratic?" *Ancient Philosophy* 10 (1990): 1–16.

________. "Reasons and Causes in the 'Phaedo.'" *Philosophical Review* 78 (1969): 291–325.

Listing Internet Sources

Internet sources are relatively new in the world of scholarship, and conventions are still developing. Whichever format you use, be consistent (don't shift your citation style from one entry to another) and provide enough information for the reader to locate your source.

The model presented here is similar to the MLA style. It has the following elements:

1. Author's name: Last name first. If there is no author, the name of an editor, compiler, or translator may be placed here, followed by *Ed., Comp.,* or *Trans.*
2. Title of article or Web page: within quotation marks.
3. Title of the complete website: as it appears on the home page.
4. Name of an editor, compiler, or translator, preceded by *Ed., Comp.,* or *Trans.:* If not cited in place of the author at the beginning of the entry.
5. Version or volume number.
6. Date of publication.
7. Total number of pages, paragraphs, or sections: enter "n. pag" if a lengthy source has "no pagination" and no other way to indicate length.
8. Organization or institution associated with the site.
9. Date accessed.
10. URL in pointed brackets.

An Article within a Reference Volume

Oliver, Amy. "Latin American Philosophy." *Routledge Encyclopedia of Philosophy.* 1996. Six para. 10 January 1999 <http://www.thomson.com/rcenters/philres/rep/latin.html>

An Article with an Author and an Editor

Millgram, Elijah. "Practical Reasoning." *Dictionary of the Philosophy of Mind.* Ed. Chris Eliasmith. 31 para. 10 January 1999 <http://artsci.wustl.edu/~philos/MindDict/practicalreasoning.html#maieutic>

A Citation with a Sponsoring/Associated Institution

Toadvine, Theodore A., Comp. "Simone de Beauvoir & Existential Phenomenology: A Bibliography." *Center for Advanced Research in Phenomenology.* 21 March 1998. 15 sections. Florida Atlantic University. 30 January 1999 <http://www.flinet.com/carp/simone1.htm>

A Scholarly Journal

Jaggar, Alison M. "Globalizing Feminist Ethics." *Hypatia* 13.2 (Spring 1998): 7 sections. 30 January 1999 <http:viator.ucs.indiana.edu/~iupress/journals/hyp13-2.htm>

To decide how to create an entry for an unusual printed resource or for nonprint resources, consult the *MLA Handbook for Writers of Research Papers,* 6th edition, by Joseph Gibaldi and Walter S. Achtert (New York: Modern Language Association, 2003).

DOCUMENTATION WITH FOOTNOTES OR ENDNOTES

For many people, the most familiar form of documentation for specific passages in a paper is the use of notes—footnotes or endnotes. Footnotes are located at the bottom of the page on which the reference is cited. Endnotes appear at the end of the paper. Notes are signaled in the text of the paper by a superscript number, raised above the line of type at the end of the passage that requires the reference. Because the information in a reference note is similar to the information in a bibliographic entry, bibliographies are sometimes omitted when notes are used. Still, many professors expect both.

Reference notes have four elements: (1) author's name, (2) title of the work, (3) publication information, and (4) page reference.

Citing Books: First Reference

The initial note referring to each book takes a standard form that provides full identification of the book. Subsequent references to the same book are much briefer, and will be discussed later in this chapter.

A Book by One Author

1. Mary Whitlock Blundell, *Helping Friends and Harming Enemies: A Study in Sophocles and Greek Ethics* (Cambridge: Cambridge University Press, 1989) 207.

A Book with Coauthors

2. Schuyler W. Huck and Howard M. Sandler, *Rival Hypotheses: Alternative Interpretations of Data Based Conclusions* (New York: Harper & Row, 1979) 11, 158.

An Anthology of Collected Work

3. F. S. C. Northrop and Mason W. Gross, *Alfred North Whitehead: An Anthology* (New York: Macmillan, 1961) 9.

An Article in an Anthology

4. Julius Moravcsik, "Learning as Recollection," *Plato*, ed. Gregory Vlastos, vol. 1 (Garden City: Anchor-Doubleday, 1971) 54–55.

A Book with an Author, a Translator, and an Editor

5. Gottfried Wilhelm von *Leibniz, Leibniz: Discourse on Metaphysics, Correspondence with Arnauld, and Monadology*, trans. George R. Montgomery, ed. Eugene Freeman (LaSalle: Open Court, 1968) 28.

A Multivolume Work

6. Frederick Copleston, *A History of Philosophy*, vol. 8 part 2 (Garden City: Image-Doubleday, 1967) 199–205.

A Book in a Series

7. Thomas S. Kuhn, *The Structure of Scientific Revolutions*, International Encyclopedia of Unified Science ser 2.2 (Chicago: University of Chicago Press, 1962) 35–36.

A Book in Another Language

8. Hermann Gundert, *Dialog und Dialektik: Zur Struktur des platonischen Dialogs* [Dialogue and Dialectic: On the Structure of the Platonic Dialogues] (Amsterdam: Verlag B. R. Gruner N. V., 1971) 48.

An Introduction, Preface, Foreword, Afterword, or Appendix

9. Martin Ostwald, translator's introduction, *Nicomachean Ethics* by Aristotle (Indianapolis: Bobbs-Merrill, 1962) xxii.

An Article in a Reference Work

10. "Alcibiades," *Who Was Who in the Greek World*, 1984 ed.

Citing Articles: First Reference

A Magazine Article

11. Don S. Rice and Prudence M. Rice, "Collapse to Contact: Post-classic Archaeology of the Peten Maya," *Archaeology* Mar.–Apr. 1984: 46–51.

A Newspaper Article

12. Ellen K. Coughlin, "New Access to Scrolls Is Unlikely to Settle Scholarly Dispute," *Chronicle of Higher Education* 6 November 1991: A9.

A Scholarly Journal

13. Anne Boykin and Savina O. Schoenhofer, "Story as Link between Nursing Practice, Ontology, Epistemology," *Image: Journal of Nursing Scholarship* 23 (1991): 245–246.

14. Joyce Trebilcot, "Sex Roles: The Argument from Nature," *Ethics* 85 (1975) 250.

15. Sanford Pinsker, "Revisionist Thought, Academic Power, and the Aging American Intellectual," *The Gettysburg Review* 3 (1990): 420.

16. Jorge J. E. Gracia, "Philosophical Analysis in Latin America," *History of Philosophy Quarterly* 1 (1984): 112.
17. Annette Baier, "Mixing Memory and Desire," *American Philosophical Quarterly* 13 (1976): 213–214.

Citing the Internet

Here are a few samples of footnote/endnote documentation for Internet sites. As with the print sources, the author's first name precedes the last name, and commas separate citation elements rather than periods. The date is to identify recency of the creation or revision of the site.

A Professor's Article Published on the World Wide Web

18. Tad Beckman, "Martin Heidegger and Environmental Ethics," <http://thuban.ac.hmc.edu/~tbeckman/personal/Heidart.html>, 1997.

A Scholarly Journal

19. Sasha Torres, "War and Remembrance: Televisual Narrative, National Memory, and *China Beach," Camera Obscura* 33–34, <http://www.indiana.edu/~iupress/journals/cam33-34.html>, special issue [no date].

An Article in a Reference Volume

20. "Virtue Theory," Internet Encyclopedia of Philosophy, Ed. James Fieser, <http://www.utm.edu/research/iep/v/virtue.htm>, 1998.

Second and Subsequent References to Books and Articles

After the first reference, the notes are easy to write. The last name of the author or authors, followed by the page number for the new reference, is sufficient. Here are some examples:

21. Baier 220.
22. Boykin and Schoenhofer 247.
23. Trebilcot 251.

If more than one work by a single author or by coauthors has already been cited, you must be specific enough in your second reference to identify the correct source. Usually a key word or phrase from the title will serve the purpose. Here are examples:

24. Kant, *Prolegomena* 50–51.
25. Kant, *Pure Reason* 107, 113.

The first of the two Kant references is to his *Prolegomena to Any Future Metaphysics.* The second reference is to his *Critique of Pure Reason.* You may use the entire title, *Critique of Pure Reason,* instead of the abbreviation. Note that the example avoids the abbreviation *Critique*, since Kant also published the *Critique of Practical Reason* and the *Critique of Judgment*. Certainly, if either of these two other titles had been referenced earlier in the same paper, the abbreviation *Critique* would be an inappropriate choice.

COMMENTARY NOTES

Notes at the foot of a page or at the end of the paper may also be used for commentary by the author when the remarks are a sidelight to the development of the ideas in the paper or would disrupt the flow of those ideas. The notes may be short or long.

Charlotte L. Stough, in her previously referred to article (see page 76) in the journal *Phronesis* (21.1), employs many of these commentary notes. Here is one of them:

39. My argument in this section has been a negative one. It has not been my intention to offer a detailed interpretation of the text from 103d to the end of the immortality argument. That complicated passage raises more questions than I could hope to deal with in this paper. Instead I have focused on a single problem which bears directly on my thesis with the aim of showing that nothing in Plato's language there commits him to a tripartite ontology. Given these limitations of objective, the thesis set forth in this paper will be compatible with more than one interpretation of that passage.

In many of Stough's notes, she combines commentary and reference to another work. Her forty-second note is an example of this:

42. My conclusion in its most general form thus accords with Paul Shorey's contention that in the *Phaedo* Plato "is really describing a possible procedure of logic and not a false a priori method of the investigation of nature" ("The Origin of the Syllogism," *Classical Philology* 19 (1924) #8).

Stough's last note, placed at the very end of the last paragraph of her paper, is used to acknowledge support:

44. Most of the work for this paper was done while I held a fellowship at the Center for Hellenic Studies in Washington, D.C., which I gratefully acknowledge. A similar version of the paper was presented at the December, 1973 meeting of the Society for Ancient Greek Philosophy in Atlanta, Georgia.

Students in philosophy classes may augment their papers with commentary notes for clarification or additional observation, but they should not use them for personal remarks about their preparation or understanding of the material or assignment. Here is a sample of a student's commentary note:

22. The expression "critically analyze" is used here to describe a process in which a person attempts to discern (1) the intention of the original author, as well as (2) strengths and weaknesses in that author's reasoning.

This definition of an important expression might be included in the body of the student's paper. The student must decide whether placement in the main text or a commentary note is more appropriate.

PARENTHETICAL DOCUMENTATION

The Modern Language Association of America, known as the MLA, has refined a system of parenthetical documentation. With this system, documentary notes—footnotes or endnotes—are unnecessary. The bibliography, now known as the list of "works cited," gives author, title, and publishing information for each work cited. Consequently, the only thing required is a way to flag the correct entry for readers as they progress through the paper—and a specific page number each time such a reference is made. With this system, the only notes that remain are the commentary notes with special remarks for the reader.

In a paper, parenthetical documentation should be placed wherever a reference is made to one of the works cited. Usually, only the page number or numbers of the cited passage need to be put in parentheses. If more information is necessary for clarity, add it. Additional information may include the author's name, the title, the volume number, or the name of a section of the book.

To refer to an entire work, without specific focus on a certain part or passage, simply use the author's name. Do not use only a title; the works cited are listed by author. A reader's quick check for the entry will be easier if you identify the author. If the author is not mentioned in the sentence that requires acknowledgment, place the author's name in parentheses. If the author has more than one work cited on the list, then write a short form of the title in parentheses.

> Dewey placed the work of art in the human psyche and distinguished between active and passive phases in the aesthetic consciousness. [One work by Dewey listed in Works Cited]
>
> On the other hand, the work of art has been placed, through definition, in the human psyche (Dewey) rather than in the object. [One work by Dewey listed in Works Cited; Dewey not named in sentence]
>
> Despite his taste for writing novels and plays, Sartre was also capable of philosophical system-building *(Being)*. [More than one work by Sartre listed in Works Cited]

To refer to certain pages or a specific part of a work (e.g., introduction), place the page number(s) or part name in parentheses. If the author has not been named, precede the page number with the author's name. If more than one work by the author is on the list of works cited, name the work before giving the page number and enclose them together in parentheses.

> Tillich distinguishes between symbols and signs (41–43). [One work by Tillich listed in Works Cited]

It is not a recent insight that "it is a common failing of mortals to deem the more difficult the fairer" (Descartes 29). [One work by Descartes listed in Works Cited]

It is not a recent insight that "it is a common failing of mortals to deem the more difficult the fairer" (Descartes, *Rules* 29). [More than one work by Descartes listed in Works Cited]

Descartes observed that "it is a common failing of mortals to deem the more difficult the fairer" (*Rules 29*). [More than one work by Descartes listed in Works Cited; Descartes named in sentence]

For a multivolume work, the volume number and a colon should precede the page number.

Leibniz's work was not well known by Berkeley (Matson 2:347). [One work by Matson listed in Works Cited; Matson not named in sentence]

Matson claims that Leibniz's work was not well known by Berkeley (2:347). [One work by Matson listed in Works Cited; Matson named in sentence]

An exact quote or a paraphrase that is derived from a secondary source may be cited, but the symbol *qtd. in* must be used in the parenthetical documentation. Even vague reference to the quoted material may be made in this way.

Julian Huxley claimed that the mind-body problem must be approached from what he called "the evolutionary angle" (qtd. in Russell 3:249).

It is also possible to refer to two sources in one parenthetical reference. Simply separate the two with a semicolon.

Theophrastus, in writing the history of the pre-Socratics, assimilated the biases of Aristotle rather than assessing the evidence freshly, with the possibility of coming to original conclusions (Allen 26–27; Kirk and Raven 3–4).

Again, for documentation rules that cover cases not examined here, consult the *MLA Handbook for Writers of Research Papers*.

OTHER SYSTEMS OF DOCUMENTATION

The number system of documentation is a variety of parenthetical documentation. The listings in Works Cited are numbered in series. The entries may be ordered alphabetically, chronologically, or according to any other plan. In each set of documentary parentheses, the number of the work is cited instead of the author's name. The number, sometimes underlined, is followed by a comma and the page number.

In another system, called in-text citation, the person who writes the paper provides all reference information in the body of the paper. Neither a list of works cited nor documentary notes is used. Papers with very few references are the most likely candidates for this method. The form is basically bibliographic, but commas replace periods.

> Philip Rahv, in his introduction to *Selected Stories of Franz Kafka* (New York: Modern-Random, 1952), identifies *In the Penal Colony* as a transition between the early works in which the principle of authority has the form of a familial father and the later works in which that principle has been "generalized into an institutional power."
>
> With a Socratic lament for those who give up the fight to develop a strong moral character, Marcus Aurelius wrote, "It is a shame when the soul is first to give way in this life, and the body does not give way" (*Meditations*, Roslyn, NY: Walter J. Black, 1945).

A SPECIAL CONSIDERATION FOR USING INTERNET SOURCES

Sometimes, the writer of a paper saves sections of text from one or more websites, then places them in the paper being written without remembering to cite the source. Thus, the material is inappropriately presented as the paper writer's own. This mistake can be avoided by saving and "pasting" into your paper others' passages **in a different font** than your own. After you have written the citation of the source or acknowledged the source within the text of your paper, and added quotation marks, you should change to one consistent font.

Appendix A

Editing Your Paper

In this appendix, you will find critiqued excerpts of various papers, and revised versions of those excerpts. In many cases there is more than one way to correct a specific writing problem. The revised version will illustrate one of those ways.

First, consider an opening paragraph from a paper on Plato's *Republic.*

Underline or italicize a book title.

Plato's Republic has been considered by many scholars[1] to be intended as a blueprint for an ideal society. A blueprint in the sense that he would like all societies to be structured exactly as he has described in the book. I will contend that Plato intended only to identify perennial causes of conflict and corruption in societies, to articulate the extreme means that would be required to eliminate this kind of conflict all together; and to leave it up to the leaders or citizens of each society to reflect on the extent to which such measures are desirable. To support this thesis, I will (1) Show that a didactic statement of truths is uncharacteristic of Plato's writings generally. (2) From the point in Book II at which Socrates balks at developing the city beyond its "city of pigs" stage, he is suggesting having reservations about these proposed controls. Perhaps this is partly because he doesn't consider them to be unqualifiedly desirable. (3) He actually denies the possibility of people with the characteristics of a philosopher king. (4) The banishment of artist's from the city is an unlikely position for Plato to take.

This is not a complete sentence.

altogether

No semicolon here (see p. 51).

Use lowercase.

awkward phrasing

Can you be more concise on #2?

This series doesn't have parallel construction.

Use plural form here—not possessive.

The author rewrote this passage, eliminating the indicated problems. The revision looked like this.

> Plato's *Republic* has been considered by many scholars[1] to be intended as a blueprint for an ideal society. This blueprint concept suggests that Plato would like all societies to be structured exactly as the one he has described. I will contend that Plato intended only to identify perennial causes of conflict and corruption in societies, to articulate the extreme means that would be required to eliminate this kind of conflict altogether, and to leave it up to the leaders or citizens of each society to reflect on the extent to which such measures are desirable. To support this thesis, I will (1) show that a didactic statement of truths is uncharacteristic of Plato's writings generally, (2) interpret Socrates' balk at developing the city beyond its "city of pigs" stage as a sign of his reservations about the proposals for a more complex city, (3) remind the reader of Plato's implicit denial of the possibility of people with the characteristics of a philosopher king, and (4) present the banishment of artists from the city as an unlikely position for Plato to take.

In the revised version, the author has italicized the book title. The second sentence has been transformed from a sentence fragment into a complete sentence, with subject and predicate. The spelling error has been corrected. The semicolon has been replaced with a comma. The author was referred to Chapter 5, "Language," in *Writing Philosophy Papers,* and discovered, or was reminded, that an independent clause (a complete statement with subject and predicate) must both precede and follow a semicolon. The preview of the series of supporting points for the thesis was reworded so that each point was made in a way that was grammatically similar to the others. An adjustment to lowercase was made following the number (1). Point (2) was made more compact. Finally, the apostrophe was eliminated from the plural noun *artists*.

Now consider a passage from a paper on René Descartes's *Meditations*.

Be consistent with verb tense.

Descartes never claimed that an "evil genius not less powerful than deceitful" (Haldane 148) actually exists. He only claims, in the first Meditation, that we cannot establish "one hundred per cent" that such a being does not exist. For Descartes, this is enough. He only needs to establish the POSSIBILITY in order to throw into doubt even the seemingly certain truths of mathematics.

too colloquial

comma splice

In formal writing, avoid putting entire words in "CAPS." For emphasis, underline or italicize.

The passage was revised, and this was the result.

> Descartes never claimed that an "evil genius not less powerful than deceitful" (Haldane 148) actually exists. He only claimed, in the first Meditation, that we cannot establish with certainty that such a being does not exist. For Descartes, this is enough. He only needs to establish the *possibility* in order to throw into doubt even the seemingly certain truths of mathematics.

In the revision, the author corrects the distracting shift in verb tense. (The problem of shifting back and forth between present and past tense in discussions of historical thinkers is a common one.) The offhand phrase "one hundred per cent," which is too casual in tone for most academic papers, is reworded to *with certainty*. In the comma splice, two sentences are joined with only a comma. This punctuation is too weak. A period replaces that comma (between the words *exist* and *for*) in the revised draft. The new sentence now begins with a capital, and "him" is replaced with *Descartes,* so there is no misunderstanding, even on first reading, about the antecedent of the deleted pronoun (*him*). "POSSIBILITY" is changed to "*possibility*." Three other small changes are made: *a* is changed to *an* in the first sentence of the passage, the "typo" error in the last sentence is corrected, and *mathematics* is written out. (Note: Parenthetical documentation is used in this example. Footnote/endnote documentation had been used in the preceding example.)

Here is a passage from a paper on the pre-Socratic philosophers.

both

The pre-Socratic atomists had discovered a way to acknowledge the basic claim of Parmenides and the basic claim of Heraclitus. The atoms themselves were eternal and indestructable. Thus, reality was essentially changeless, according to the atomists. This was in accordance with Parmenide's basic claim. At the same time, the interim combinations of atoms (in the forms of rocks, wood, flesh, and other physical substances) would come into being and pass away. Thus, Heraclitus's dictum that "panta rhei", everything ~~changes~~, is recognized as true also. In this way, pre-Socratic naturalistic philosophy resolved it's own supposedly irreconcilable dichotomy.

spelling

Is there a better word?

flows (changes),

it's - contraction of "it is"
its - possessive pronoun ("belonging to it")

The revised passage looks like this.

> The pre-Socratic atomists had discovered a way to acknowledge both the basic claim of Parmenides and the basic claim of Heraclitus. The atoms themselves were eternal and indestructible. Thus, reality was essentially changeless, according to the atomists. This was in accordance with Parmenides' basic claim. At the same time, the temporary combinations of atoms (in the forms of rocks, wood, flesh, and other physical substances) would come into being and pass away. Thus, Heraclitus's dictum that "panta rhei," *everything flows* (*changes*), is recognized as true also. In this way, pre-Socratic naturalistic philosophy resolved its own supposedly irreconcilable dichotomy.

The addition of the word *both* is not grammatically necessary, but it emphasizes the opposition of the two schools of thought referred to in the sentence. The author has spelled *indestructible* correctly after consulting a dictionary or running a spellchecker. *Parmenides'* is one correct possessive form for the name Parmenides, although *Parmenides's* is preferred by some authorities on language usage. In the new draft, *temporary* replaces *interim,* which has an awkwardly modern sound to it and implies a one-time "in between" stage. (Sometimes an awkward substitution is made when a writer rashly selects a "synonym" from a thesaurus.) The comma should precede the quotation mark in "panta rhei." The phrase *everything flows* (*changes*) might have been placed within quotation marks if the preceding transliteration of the Greek had not already been placed in quotation marks. There is still a need, however, to identify *everything flows* (*changes*) as a phrase under discussion rather than as the author's own words. Italics serve that purpose here. Underlining would be acceptable also. Finally, the apostrophe is now deleted in the last sentence, as it should be.

Now consider part of a paper about the political philosophy of John Locke, the seventeenth-century English thinker.

This is a sample in which something more than simple editing is required. The author needs to rewrite the last several sentences to eliminate the unpolished, imprecise style.

> Locke wrote that humans have inalienable rights: a right to life, a right to liberty, and a right to property. The rights to life and liberty are substantial ones, as Locke describes them in his *The Second Treatise of Government*, guaranteeing tangible benefits to its claimants. The right to property, however, may appear at first, to a reader of this treatise, to guarantee more than it ultimately does. Locke does not diverge so radically from his background as a person of the propertied class so that he actually becomes an economic egalitarian. His final position on the right to property is that not everyone is guaranteed actual possessions. The right is to compete in the economic marketplace for property; no one may deprive you by statute or by edict of your place in the free market of economic rivals.

The quotation marks in the first sentence are deleted in the revision. *Inalienable* is a nontechnical English word that is used in its conventional sense, so the quotation marks are unnecessary. The three sentence fragments that follow are now included in the opening sentence. In the next sentence, the book title is italicized instead of being placed in quotation marks. The vague word *strong* is deleted and the point is clarified with the word *substantial* and the explanatory phrase that now follows the book title. The last part of the paragraph is completely redrafted. Notice that the spelling error in the second line from the bottom of the earlier draft would not have been flagged by a conventional spellchecker because the spelling is correct for a different word. Notice also that, in the first draft, the word *right* was mistakenly omitted in one of the sentences. Also notice that, in the revision, the semicolon (in the last sentence) is used correctly. An independent clause—a complete statement with subject and predicate, able to stand alone—both precedes and follows the semicolon.

Appendix B

Sample Paper with Documentation

The following is a short sample paper with parenthetical documentation. After you take note of this now popular documentation format, examine the subsequent excerpt from the same paper, which is presented in a traditional footnote format.

A Consistent Socrates:
Justice, Gods, and the State

Fred Bolger

Knowledge and Reality
Philosophy 101
Palomar College
September 12, 2008

1

In Plato's *Apology*, Socrates tells the court that he will never stop practicing philosophy, even if the court or state orders him to stop. Then, in Plato's *Crito*, Socrates says he can't escape from prison, even to save his life, because he would be violating the laws of the state. At first glance, the old philosopher would appear to be contradicting himself. Socrates' statements, however, can be shown to be consistent. This can be shown within the context of his commitment to living a good or just life, his constant desire to please the gods, and his love for the state of Athens.

The first context within which we can show the consistency of Socrates' two apparently conflicting claims is his commitment to living a just life. In the *Apology*, Socrates suggests that he wants to be just when he states, "I thought that it was my duty to face it out on the side of law and justice rather than support you, through fear of prison or death, in your decision" (56).

Socrates again suggests that he wants to be just when he says, "I do not think that it is just for a man to appeal to the jury or to get himself acquitted doing so . . ." (*Apology* 60). Again, Socrates refuses to do something that he sees as unjust. He refuses to do it even though he could probably thereby save his own life. Since Socrates would rather die than be unjust, we can conclude that he would rather do anything than lead an unjust life.

When Socrates states that he went "like a father or an elder brother to see each one of you privately, . . . urging you to set your thoughts on goodness" (*Apology* 55), he shows that he was honestly trying to do good by philosophizing. He had led a good and reflective life, and was trying to help others do the same.He had seen it as his duty to help the people of Athens lead good lives. Thus, he provides a valuable service to the Athenians. Socrates sees this service as a greater good than the good that could be accomplished by his following the state's hypothetical order to stop practicing philosophy.

Socrates shows that he is also trying to be just by staying in prison when he asks rhetorically: "Ought one to fulfill all one's agreements, provided that they are just, or break them?" (*Crito* 85). The particular agreement he has in mind is the agreement to live by the laws of Athens. By leaving prison without the consent of the state he would be breaking the law. By breaking the law he would be breaking his agreement with Athens. In breaking this

2

agreement, he would be committing an injustice. Thus, he concludes that by escaping prison he would be committing an unjust act.

The second context within which Socrates can be shown to have been consistent, and not contradictory, is his eagerness to please the gods. He shows that he feels that the gods want him to philosophize when he observes that it would be a strange thing if, when facing death during the war, he remained at his post, like his fellow warriors, "and yet afterwards, when God appointed me, as I supposed and believed, to the duty of leading the philosophic life, examining myself and others, I were then through fear of death or of any other danger to desert my post" (*Apology* 52). Socrates clearly claims that practicing philosophy is a divinely imposed duty for him. He feels that nothing should dissuade him from carrying out this duty. He suggests a battlefront comparison: no matter what happens, you must stay at your post and carry out your duties. So, even though he will probably die, Socrates can't forsake his post in Athens and agree to stop practicing philosophy. Since he wants to please the gods, he is willing to die rather than abandon philosophy.

Socrates also declines the offer to escape prison because he feels that it is what would please the gods most. He says, "[Y]ou must do whatever your city and country commands . . . but violence against your mother or father is an unholy act and it is a far greater sin against your country" (*Crito* 87). The words "unholy" and "sin" imply defiance of one's gods. He suggests here that the gods want him to follow his country's commands. Since Athens commands him to go to prison and die for his "crimes," then, Socrates would transgress on his gods' wishes if he were to do otherwise.

This could also be why he declares, in the *Apology*, his unwillingness to stop philosophizing. He is precluding just such a court ban in order to avoid a situation in which he would have to actually make the choice between the authority of the state and that of the gods. He feels he must avoid displeasing the gods at all costs.

The third context in which to understand Socrates's apparently conflicting claims in the *Apology* and in the *Crito* is his love of Athens. Socrates believes that by philosophizing he is actually helping the state that he loves. He explains this to the court through a simile. He says, "To put it bluntly (even if it sounds rather comical), God has assigned me to this city; as if to a large

3

thoroughbred horse which because of its great size is inclined to be lazy and needs the stimulation of some stinging fly" (*Apology* 54). Socrates portrays himself as the fly and Athens as the horse. He suggests that Athens needs him to stimulate it. If the fly is removed, the horse will luxuriate in its laziness, and not be the noble steed it could be. Thus, in order to save the city he loves, he must continue to stimulate it—that is, to philosophize. He thus characterizes himself as a necessary irritant.

His love of the state can also explain his resolution to remain in prison. He asks, "Do you imagine that a city can continue to exist and not be turned upside down, if the legal judgments which are pronounced in it have no force but are nullified by private persons?" (*Crito* 86). He implies that if he were to escape from prison he would, at the least, weaken Athens. This demonstrates his love of Athens: he would rather die than hurt his city. He continued to love Athens even after it had sentenced him to die.

In conclusion, we can now acquit Socrates of the charge that he was inconsistent in declaring first, to the court, that he would not cease his public philosophical activities even if he were to be ordered to do so by the state, and by insisting, only days later, that a prison escape would be wrong because of his duty to obey the laws of his state. This acquittal has been justified with reference to Plato's accounts of Socrates' own remarks, and considering three contexts: his commitment to a just life, his desire to please the gods, and his love for the state of Athens.

4

Works Cited

Plato. *Apology*. Trans. Hugh Tredennick and Harold Tarrant. *The Last Days of Socrates.* New York: Penguin, 1993.

Plato. Crito. Trans. Hugh Tredennick and Harold Tarrant. *The Last Days of Socrates*. New York: Penguin, 1993.

In the preceding student paper, the references in the body of the paper (in parentheses) to the Works Cited include author, title, and page number. The title, or an abbreviation of it, is included here only because there is more than one work by Plato to be cited. If a reference to Xenophon's *Recollections of Socrates* had been a third cited source, and the only source by Xenophon, then the parenthetical reference would include only Xenophon's name and the page number. As with the other two sources, the specific publication information, indicating which edition of the *Recollections* had been used, would be provided on the Works Cited page.

On the following pages, you can see how the beginning part of this paper would appear if footnotes had been used instead of parenthetical documentation.

1

In Plato's *Apology*, Socrates tells the court that he will never stop practicing philosophy, even if the court or state orders him to stop. Then, in Plato's *Crito*, Socrates says he can't escape from prison, even to save his life, because he would be violating the laws of the state. At first glance, the old philosopher would appear to be contradicting himself. Socrates' statements, however, can be shown to be consistent. This can be shown within the context of his commitment to living a good or just life, his constant desire to please the gods, and his love for the state of Athens.

The first context within which we can show the consistency of Socrates' two apparently conflicting claims is his commitment to living a just life. In the *Apology*, Socrates demonstrates that he wants to be just when he states, "I thought that it was my duty to face it out on the side of law and justice rather than support you, through fear of prison or death, in your decision."[1]

Socrates again shows that he wants to be just when he says, "I do not think that it is just for a man to appeal to the jury or to get himself acquitted doing so . . ."[2] Again, Socrates refuses to do something that he sees as unjust. He refuses to do it even though he could probably thereby save his own life. Since Socrates would rather die than be unjust, we can conclude that he would rather do anything than lead an unjust life.

When Socrates states that he went "like a father or an elder brother to see each one of you privately, . . . urging you to set your thoughts on goodness,"[3] he shows that he was honestly trying to do good by philosophizing. He had led a good and reflective life, and was trying to help others do the same. He had seen it as his duty to help the people of Athens lead good lives. Thus, he provides a valuable service to the Athenians. Socrates sees this service as a greater good than the good that could be accomplished by his following the state's hypothetical order to stop practicing philosophy.

Socrates shows that he is also trying to be just by staying in prison when he asks rhetorically: "Ought one to fulfill all one's agreements, provided that they are just, or break them?"[4] The particular agreement he has in mind is the agreement to live by the laws of Athens. By leaving prison without the consent of the state he would be breaking the law. By breaking the law he would be

2

breaking his agreement with Athens. In breaking this agreement, he would be committing an injustice. Thus, he concludes that by escaping prison he would be committing an unjust act.

The second context within which Socrates can be shown to have been consistent, and not contradictory, is his eagerness to please the gods. He shows that he feels that the gods want him to philosophize when he observes that it would be a strange thing if, when facing death during the war, he remained at his post, like his fellow warriors, "and yet afterwards, when God appointed me, as I supposed and believed, to the duty of leading the philosophic life, examining myself and others, I were then through fear of death or of any other danger to desert my post."[5] Socrates clearly claims that practicing philosophy is a divinely imposed duty for him. He feels that nothing should dissuade him from carrying out this duty. He suggests a battlefront comparison: no matter what happens, you must stay at your post and carry out your duties. So, even though he will probably die, Socrates can't forsake his post in Athens and agree to stop practicing philosophy. Since he wants to please the gods, he is willing to die rather than abandon philosophy.

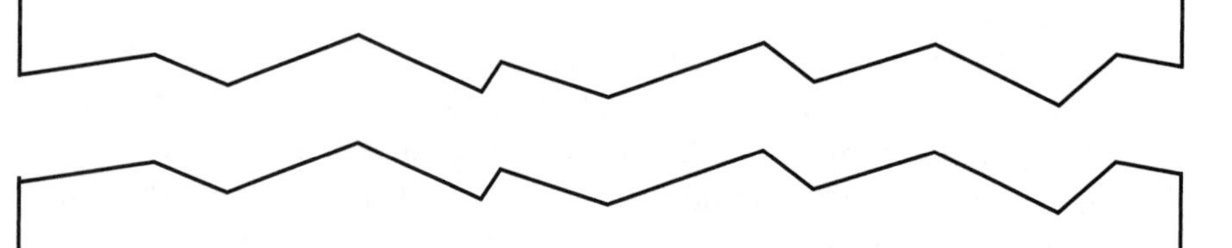

[1]Plato, *Apology*, trans. Hugh Tredennick and Harold Tarrant, *The Last Days of Socrates* (New York: Penguin, 1993) 56.

[2]Plato 60.

[3]Plato 55.

[4]Plato, *Crito*, trans. Hugh Tredennick and Harold Tarrant, *The Last Days of Socrates* (New York: Penguin, 1993) 85.

[5]Plato, *Apology* 52.

Appendix C

Formal Patterns of Logic

Deductive patterns of reasoning are the forms of argumentation in which the premises are designed to "necessarily" establish the conclusion. If you want to review the concepts argument, premise, and conclusion before dealing with them in this appendix, please turn to pages 13–15.

VALIDITY AND SOUNDNESS

Sometimes a writer suggests that if the reader accepts the premises that have been offered, then the reader has no logical alternative to accepting the conclusion also. If the writer's reasoning is successful—that is, if the premises do lead *necessarily* to the conclusion—logicians would label the argument as a **valid** one.

To decide whether the reasoning in an argument is valid (whether the evidence proves the conclusion), it is not necessary to concern yourself with the question of whether the premises are true. You can ignore the truth or falsity of the premises and still determine whether the argument is valid. *In a valid argument, if the premises were true, then the conclusion would have to be true.* This means that although the premises may or may not actually be true, you should *imagine* that they are, then ask if that shows beyond any possibility of doubt that the conclusion must be true. In other words, to determine whether an argument is valid, you ask, "If the premises were true, would the conclusion then have to be true?" A "yes" answer to this question indicates that the argument is valid. An answer of "no" or "maybe," or even "probably," indicates that the argument is not valid, a condition logicians describe by saying the argument is *invalid.*

Consider two more definitions of validity. They present the preceding point in different words.

1. An argument is valid when it is inconceivable for the premises to be true while the conclusion is false.
2. An argument is valid if, by accepting the evidence, we must also (to avoid contradicting ourselves) accept the conclusion.

The reasoning in the following argument would be valid, and the argument will be called a valid one, even though one of the premises is false.

> Utopian states must be possible because the creation of a utopian state is desirable, and anything that is desirable is possible.

The conclusion, "Utopian states must be possible," is stated at the beginning of the argument. The argument is valid because *if* the premises were true, then the conclusion would have to be true. The argument has a good inference; its premises establish its conclusion with necessity. However, since at least one premise, "anything that is desirable is possible," is almost certainly false, the argument does not have good evidence. This is not an acceptable argument, even though the reasoning is valid.

The following argument is also valid:

> Since all historically important philosophers have been Germans, and any German is an extremely systematic thinker, all historically important philosophers have been extremely systematic thinkers.

The conclusion is stated last. Both premises in this argument are false, but the argument is valid because *if* it were true that all historically important philosophers have been Germans and *if* it were true that any German is an extremely systematic thinker, *then* it would necessarily be true that all historically important philosophers have been extremely systematic thinkers.

Consider another argument:

> Martin Heidegger must be an extremely systematic thinker because he's an influential German philosopher and most influential German philosophers are systematic thinkers.

This argument is invalid because *even if* Martin Heidegger is an influential German philosopher and *even if* most influential German philosophers are systematic thinkers, this would not prove that Heidegger is one of those (in the "most" group) who are extremely systematic thinkers. Notice that you might believe—or even *know* on other evidence—that the conclusion is true; you still would have to admit that the argument presented here is invalid.

To decide whether an argument is sound (and thus whether the conclusion must be accepted), you must determine whether it passes both of the following tests:

1. The argument must be valid.
2. All premises must be true.

Test 1 requires that the evidence actually prove the conclusion. Test 2 requires that the evidence be reliable evidence. Obviously, when reliable evidence proves the conclusion, that conclusion should be accepted as true. The argument has both a good inference (it has passed the first test) and good evidence (it has passed the second test). If the argument fails either test, it is unsound.

Call to mind the first two arguments used in the explanation of validity.

> Utopian states must be possible because the creation of a utopian state is desirable, and anything that is desirable is possible.

> Since all historically important philosophers have been Germans, and any German is an extremely systematic thinker, all historically important philosophers have been extremely systematic thinkers.

Both arguments were valid; the conclusion followed from the premises. Thus, they pass the first test for soundness. However, at least one premise in each argument is false. Thus, each argument fails the second test for soundness. Although these arguments have a good inference, they do not have good evidence.

The following argument is sound:

> All philosophers who endorse Kantian ethics believe that respect for persons should be accepted as a basic ethical principle, and no one who believes that (respect for persons should be accepted as a basic ethical principle) can consistently support hate crime. Thus, any philosopher who endorses Kantian ethics cannot consistently support hate crime.

To check its validity, we ask: "*If* all philosophers who endorse Kantian ethics actually do believe that respect for persons should be a basic ethical principle, *and if* no one who believes that can consistently support hate crime, *then* would it have to be true that any philosopher who endorses Kantian ethics cannot consistently support hate crime?" The answer is "yes" (barring a peculiar assessment of the premises), showing that the argument is valid. This argument clearly passes the first test for soundness. The other question to be asked is this: "Are all the premises true?" Again, the answer is "yes." Since the argument passes both tests, it is sound, and the conclusion must be true.

Notice that it is possible for an argument to be valid and sound, valid and unsound, or invalid and unsound. Only one combination is impossible. It is impossible for an argument to be invalid and sound since, in order to be a sound argument, it must pass test 1, which requires it to be a valid argument. By the definitions of the terms, then, no argument can be invalid and sound. If the argument is invalid, it is necessarily unsound—you don't even need to determine whether the premises are true or false.

Notice also that unsound arguments will not always have false conclusions. For that matter, invalid arguments will not always have false conclusions. Here

Inference	Evidence or Premises	Soundness of Argument
Deductively valid	All true	Sound
	One or more false	Unsound
Deductively invalid	All true	Unsound
	One or more false	Unsound

we see an example of an argument that is invalid and therefore unsound. The conclusion, however, is true.

> Although most people are theists or agnostics, hundreds of thousands of people are atheists. Philosophers come from this larger cultural community. Certainly, then, philosophers are divided on this issue, too: some of them must be theists and some are undoubtedly atheists.

The conclusion is that some philosophers are atheists (and that others are theists). While the conclusion is true and could be firmly established with the appropriate premises, the author of this argument has drawn the conclusion on the basis of insufficient evidence. This is an invalid argument with a conclusion that happens to be true.

Finally, bear in mind that an argument is not to be considered unsound merely because *you do not know* whether a premise is true. If the argument is valid, then it is sound if the premises are true but unsound if the premises are not true. If you are not certain about whether a premise is true or false, the argument's soundness is undetermined until you look into the matter sufficiently to establish whether it is sound. Further, if you incorrectly judge a valid argument's premises to be true or false, then you will be wrong when you assess its soundness. The soundness of deductive arguments does not depend on personal perspectives.

In the section "Mapping and Outlining" in Chapter 4, you read about a distinction between (1) offering premises that directly establish the thesis statement, and (2) offering evidence for those premises (which now can be considered as conclusions also). Many subarguments might exist as parts of the overall line of reasoning (or argument) with which you support your thesis.

You can check each subargument to decide how strong it is. Good reasoning requires both that your premises are reliable and that they are sufficient to establish your conclusion. Many tricky arguments, which don't really establish the conclusion although they may appear to, include premises with the word *if* or the word *all.* Let's examine how these counterfeits might fool us.

"IF" STATEMENTS AND ARGUMENTS

It is important for us to take a special look at the question of validity in a particular kind of argument—the conditional argument. The reason is simple: Although conditional arguments are used continually in everyday reasoning, people consistently make mistakes when deciding whether the conclusion follows from the premises.

How many times do you say the word *if* in an average day? Because this little word is so familiar, we do not become especially alert to the logic involved in its use. We should. *If* is the traditional sign of a conditional statement, and conditional statements are often presented within deceptive conditional arguments.

An if-then statement such as "If the Marxist rebels are victorious, then our country is doomed" is called a **conditional statement**. Part of the statement is offered as a condition for the other part. In this example, the speaker is claiming that the existence of the condition ("the Marxist rebels are victorious") guarantees the existence of a certain result ("our country is doomed").

In a conditional statement, the phrase that follows the word *if* is called the **antecedent.** The phrase that follows the word *then* is called the **consequent** of the conditional statement. In the example, the antecedent is "the Marxist rebels are victorious" (the condition); the consequent is "our country is doomed."

Conditional statements sometimes vary from the regular if-then form. Here are three variations:

1. The word *then* may be omitted. The meaning of the statement is not changed when we say, "If the Marxist rebels are victorious, our country is doomed."
2. The word *if* may be presented in the middle of the sentence instead of at the beginning. When we say, "Our country is doomed if the Marxist rebels are victorious," the antecedent "the Marxist rebels are victorious" comes after the consequent "our country is doomed."
3. Other words, such as *when* or *whenever*, sometimes introduce the antecedent instead of *if.* The meaning of the statement "If philosophers deny common fundamental beliefs, they are known as skeptics," is basically the same as the meaning of the statements "When philosophers deny common fundamental beliefs, they are known as skeptics," and "Whenever philosophers deny common fundamental beliefs, they are known as skeptics."

Conditional arguments, by definition, involve conditional statements. Here is an example of a conditional argument:

> If there are widespread human rights violations in a society, then that society is unjust. But this society is not an unjust one because there are not widespread human rights violations here.

The first premise is a conditional statement (If there are widespread human rights violations in a society, then that society is unjust). Then the conclusion is stated (this society is not an unjust one), and another premise is stated (there are not widespread human rights violations here). Is the argument valid? No. Certainly the absence of *widespread* human rights violations is not enought to guarantee that the entire society is a fair or just one. So even if the premises were true, the conclusion might not be true. This argument does not have good form, even if it appears to at first sight.

Here is another conditional argument:

> Gandhi was apparently not a kind and thoughtful person, because if a person is kind and thoughtful, everybody else will be considerate in return, but so many other people were not considerate to him.

Here the conclusion is stated first (Gandhi was not a kind and thoughtful person). Then comes a conditional premise (if a person is kind and thoughtful, everybody else will be considerate in return) and another premise (so many other people were not considerate to him). Is this argument valid? Yes. If the premises were true, the conclusion would have to be true. So the argument passes the test for validity. Perhaps, however, this sounds like bad reasoning to you, and perhaps the previous argument sounded as if it were good reasoning. You should indeed sense something wrong with the argument, but the problem is not one of validity—it is not a lack of good form. The problem is that the argument is not sound. The problem you may sense is that the conditional premise is false. There are good grounds to doubt the truth of the statement "If a person is kind and thoughtful, everybody else will be considerate in return." Virtually all of us know through experience that this is not a true statement. The reasoning is valid; our argument is not sound because the conditional premise is false.

Validity is the thorny problem in conditional arguments, however, because even short and simple conditional arguments are regularly evaluated incorrectly in this regard. Think of how often we use conditional arguments in everyday reasoning: "If I take that course, then . . .," "If the car could be fixed by tomorrow morning, then . . .," "If you had changed your approach, then . . ."

Let's consider how mistakes are made in such reasoning and how they can be avoided. As you write your paper, then, you will be able to recognize your own invalid conditional arguments, and rewrite to eliminate the faulty reasoning. You will also be able to be specific in your criticism of others' conditional arguments.

Examine the following four arguments. They are similar in that each has the same conditional premise, but they are not identical. Each is different from the others. In each of the four cases, decide whether the argument is valid or invalid.*

1. Whenever a Cambridge philosopher writes an essay, the thesis is well-supported.
   (And) A Cambridge philosopher wrote this essay.
   (Therefore) The thesis is well-supported.
2. Whenever a Cambridge philosopher writes an essay, the thesis is well-supported.
   (And) The thesis (of this essay) is well-supported.
   (Therefore) A Cambridge philosopher wrote this essay.
3. Whenever a Cambridge philospher writes an essay, the thesis is well-supported.
   (But) This thesis is not well-supported.
   (Therefore) A Cambridge philosopher did not write this essay.
4. Whenever a Cambridge philosopher writes an essay, the thesis is well-supported.
   (But) A Cambridge philospher did not write this essay.
   (Therefore) The thesis is not well-supported.

* Notice that the conditional arguments with which we are concerned in this section have one premise that is a conditional statement and one premise that *affirms or denies* the *antecedent or consequent* of the conditional premise. The conclusion then affirms (if the nonconditional premise affirms) or denies (if the nonconditional premise denies) the other part of the conditional premise (antecedent or consequent).

Stop here. Do not read the next paragraph unless you have already determined, to your own satisfaction, whether each of the preceding arguments is valid or invalid.

Argument 1 is valid. When we accept as true the statement "Whenever a Cambridge philosopher writes an essay, the thesis is well-supported," and when we also accept as true the statement that "a Cambridge philosopher wrote this essay," we must, to avoid contradicting ourselves, accept the statement "the thesis is well-supported." If the premises were true, the conclusion would have to be true. This, of course, does not show that the argument is sound. Still, the argument *is* valid.

Argument 2 is invalid. Even if the premises were true, the conclusion might not be true because of the possibility that other philosophers might also write essays in which the thesis is supported well. This argument is actually a counterfeit of argument 1. It is a counterfeit because, while it is similar to the "real thing" (the form of the reasoning appears enough like the first version to be mistaken for it), it is unacceptable (it is invalid). In conversation, the invalid form may be mistaken for the similar-sounding valid form. Having the premises and conclusion occurring in different locations from argument to argument makes this error even easier to commit.

Argument 3 is valid. When we accept as true the statement "Whenever a Cambridge philosopher writes an essay, the thesis is well-supported," and when we also accept as true the statement that "this thesis is not well-supported," we must, to avoid contradicting ourselves, accept the statement "a Cambridge philosopher did not write this essay." If the premises were true, the conclusion would have to be true.

Argument 4 is invalid. As in the second argument, the premises do not prove the conclusion, since there may be other philosophers who support their thesis well when they write essays. Furthermore, as with the second argument, this argument (argument 4) is actually a counterfeit of the preceding argument (argument 3). It may be mistaken for that valid argument form because it is similar, but this last argument is definitely invalid.

There is one short word that, if added to arguments 2 and 4, would transform them into valid arguments. The word is *only*. People sometimes think that when they say "only if," they are merely being emphatic about their "if" statement. Actually, however, that phrase can change the whole argument. These two alternate versions (with *only if*) of the two previously invalid arguments can be seen now to be valid.

> Only if a Cambridge philosopher wrote the essay will its thesis be well-supported. (In other words: The thesis of an essay will be well-supported only if the essay was written by a Cambridge philosopher.)
> (And) The thesis (of this essay) is well-supported.
> (Therefore) A Cambridge philosopher wrote this essay.

> Only if a Cambridge philosopher wrote the essay will its thesis be well-supported.
> (But) A Cambridge philosopher did not write this essay.
> (Therefore) The thesis is not well-supported.

Now, going back to the original four sample arguments, we need a way to determine when a conditional argument is valid because, although you may have seen clearly whether each of the four arguments was valid, this is not always such an easy matter. Conditional arguments invite confusion when we fail to distinguish between form and content.

The following list parallels the previous arguments and shows the form of each argument.

1. If A, then C.
   A.
   C.
2. If A, then C.
   C.
   A.
3. If A, then C.
   Not C.
   Not A.
4. If A, then C.
   Not A.
   Not C.

Each of the original four arguments is valid or invalid because of its form. By looking at the structure of the argument rather than the content, we can tell whether a conditional argument is valid. The preceding list shows the form of each of the original arguments. The letter *A* stands for the antecedent of the conditional premise, and the letter *C* stands for the consequent of that premise.

Compare this list with the original one. To understand the second list, note the following:

- The phrase that follows the *if* of the conditional premise is represented by the letter *A* wherever it occurs in the argument. The phrase that follows the *then* of the conditional premise is represented by the letter *C* wherever it occurs in the argument.
- *Not A* represents the denial of whichever statement is represented by the letter *A; Not C* represents the denial of whichever statement is represented by the letter *C*. If, for example, *A* represents the statement "Mathematics is an exact science," then *Not A* represents the statement "Mathematics is not an exact science.". If *A* represents the statement "Physics is not an exact science" then its denial, "Physics is an exact science," is represented by *Not A*.

If you look from the second list back to the first, you will notice that, because the antecedent of the conditional premise is roughly "a Cambridge philosopher writes an essay," this statement can be represented by the letter *A*. Because this statement is also the nonconditional premise in item 1, we can use the letter *A* to represent that entire premise. Because the statement that is the consequent of the conditional premise is also the conclusion, we can use *C* to represent the entire conclusion.

Any argument with the form shown in item 1 in the second list will be a valid one, regardless of the content.

The counterfeit version of that form may be seen in item 2, where the conditional premise and the conclusion are reversed. Any argument with this form will be an invalid one, regardless of the content—that is, regardless of whether the premises are true.

When the premises precede the conclusion as in the order displayed in the example, the error in constructing the argument is seen in the nonconditional premise. With this premise, instead of affirming the antecedent of the conditional statement to produce a valid argument, we *affirm the consequent* and produce an invalid argument. The logical error that we make is called **affirming the consequent**. It is a *formal* fallacy. In other words, it is a common error that is due to the form independently of the content of the argument.

Any argument with the form shown in item 3 will be a valid one, regardless of the content.

The counterfeit version of that form may be seen in item 4, where the non-conditional premise and the conclusion are reversed. Any argument with this form will be an invalid one, regardless of the content. When the premises precede the conclusion (in the order displayed in the example), the error in constructing the argument is seen in the nonconditional premise. With this premise, instead of denying the consequent of the conditional statement to produce a valid argument, we *deny the antecedent* and produce an invalid argument. The logical error that we make is called **denying the antecedent**. Like affirming the consequent, it is a formal fallacy.

Two formal fallacies, then, are sometimes committed in conditional arguments: affirming the consequent and denying the antecedent. You should be able to recognize these when considering someone else's reasoning and when you are reasoning on your own.

Finally, here are the answers to three reasonable questions about conditional arguments.

1. *Are these formal fallacies common?*
   Yes. Reasoning from if-then premises is a common and casual part of everyday thinking. This makes quite notable the research suggesting that people more often than not, given certain common patterns of conditional reasoning, identify as valid arguments ones that exhibit the formal fallacies of affirming the consequent or denying the antecedent.*

2. *Do the two valid forms of conditional reasoning also have names?*
   Yes. Certainly we could name them by referring to what happens in the nonconditional premise, as we do with the invalid forms. They would then be called affirming the antecedent and denying the consequent. However, they

* In his article, "Selective Processes in Reasoning," Jonathan St. B.T. Evans refers to a 1981 Evans and Beck study that found 54 percent of the respondents accepting the reasoning of the fallacious denial of the antecedent and 53 percent accepting the affirmation of the consequent. He also refers to a 1977 Evans study that yielded 38 and 67 percent results, respectively. From Jonathan St. B.T. Evans, *Thinking and Reasoning: Psychological Approaches* (London: Routledge & Kegan Paul, 1983), pp. 135–163.

are more often known by their Latin names, *modus ponens* (item 1) and *modus tollens* (item 3).

3. *Do I need to memorize the second set of argument forms?*
   No. The list should have helped you understand the forms of conditional arguments. You do not, however, need to keep a mental picture of it in order to distinguish between valid and invalid conditional arguments. If you encounter a conditional argument of the sort that we have been examining, you need only identify the conditional premise, the nonconditional premise, and the conclusion. Then, looking at the non-conditional premise (not the conclusion!), determine first whether it is similar to the antecedent or the consequent of the conditional premise, and then whether it affirms or denies that part of the conditional premise. Then you will know whether, in the crucial nonconditional premise, the argument involves affirming the antecedent, affirming the consequent, denying the antecedent, or denying the consequent. The two errors to watch for are affirming the consequent and denying the antecedent.

"ALL" STATEMENTS AND ARGUMENTS

Like *if*, the little word *all* is used casually and often. It is used in everyday conversation and in serious writing. Think carefully when you draft this word into a paragraph of your paper, because some patterns of reasoning in which *all* or its equivalent (*every, without exception*) occurs may be invalid but nevertheless appear valid. Arguments that have a universal premise (like "*All* existentialists reject traditional notions of human nature") can be almost as misleading as the conditional arguments that are based on an "if" premise. The argument forms examined in this section are called *syllogisms.*

Syllogisms are valid argument patterns with two premises, in which the premises and conclusion can be worded to start with "all," "no," or "some," and two categories of things are compared. For example, such statements might be "All books by Dostoyevski are philosophically significant books," "No books published by Nolo Press are philosophically significant books," "Some novels are philosophically important books," and "Some rigorous thinking is not philosophical thinking."

Universal Syllogism

Although the following argument is unsound, it is valid because its pattern is that of a universal syllogism:

All English philosophers are empiricists.

(And) All empiricists are logicians.

(Therefore) All English philosophers are logicians.

By accepting these (false) premises, we bind ourselves logically to an acceptance of the conclusion.

Make up your own example of this pattern of reasoning. Here is the pattern.

All A is B (or: All A's are B's).

All B is C (or: All B's are C's).

(Therefore) All A is C (or: All A's are C's).

If you choose obviously false premises, your argument will be a silly one. Still, it will be valid.

This universal syllogism is a common pattern of reasoning, and to many people its validity will be simply obvious. However, that obvious validity can itself be a problem. Being familiar with this useful pattern, *a person may mistake a similar but invalid pattern for the valid one.* Consider another argument form in which two premises and the conclusion begin with *all.*

All A is B.

All A is C.

(Therefore) All B is C.

This is the form of one kind of invalid reasoning. Here is an argument with that form:

All English philosophers are empiricists.

All English philosophers are logicians.

(Therefore) All empiricists are logicians.

If you are at all tempted to say that this argument is valid, you can understand how careful you must be to distinguish between these two patterns of reasoning. If, however, you easily recognize its invalidity, consider whether either different argument content or the occurrence of these premises in a casual conversational setting (with parenthetical comments) might not invite error. Finally, even if you would not offer such reasoning yourself, don't be amazed if someone else does.

There is another invalid look-alike that might be mistaken for the valid universal syllogism. Here is the form:

All A is B.

All C is B.

(Therefore) All A is C.

Try to create a valid argument that has this form. You can't.

Universal-to-Particular Syllogism

The following reasoning is valid:

All of Plato's dialogues are philosophically significant writings.

(And) Some of Plato's dialogues are works characterized by humor and irony.

(Therefore) Some philosophically significant writings are works characterized by humor and irony.

The conclusion follows necessarily from the premises. In other words, if you accept those premises, then you cannot consistently deny the conclusion. It would have to be true, too. The pattern of reasoning for this universal-to-particular (or "all-to-some") syllogism goes like this:

All A is B.

Some A is C (or: Some C is A).

(Therefore) Some B is C (or: Some C is B).

The key to the valid structure is that the subject category (designated by the *A*) of the universal ("all") premise is repeated in the other premise but not in the conclusion.

An invalid counterfeit of this pattern of reasoning has similar opening words for its premises and conclusion: *all, some, some.* However, the categories are presented in a different order. The deceptive pattern is this:

All A is B.

Some B is C (or: Some C is B).

(Therefore) Some A is C.

The following reasoning follows this counterfeit pattern:

All of Plato's dialogues are philosophically significant writings.

Some philosophically significant writings are works characterized by humor and irony.

Some of Plato's dialogues are characterized by humor and irony.

Although the conclusion is true, the argument is invalid because the premises are insufficient grounds on which to believe the conclusion. You would not *contradict* yourself by accepting the premises while rejecting the conclusion. (The philosophically significant writings referred to in the second premise might all be by someone other than Plato.)

Bibliography

Austin, J. L. "A Plea for Excuses." *Philosophical Papers*. London: Oxford University Press, 1970.

Baird, Forrest E., and Walter Kaufmann. *Philosophic Classics: From Plato to Derrida*. 5th ed. Upper Saddle River, NJ: Prentice-Hall, 2007.

Chicago Manual of Style. 15th ed. Chicago: University of Chicago Press, 2003.

Copleston, Frederick. *History of Philosophy*. 11 vols. Garden City, NY: Image, Vols. 1–9. London: Continuum International, Vols. 10, 11.

Durant, Will. *The Story of Philosophy*. New York: Simon & Schuster, 1991.

Edwards, Paul, ed. *Encyclopedia of Philosophy*. New York: Macmillan, 1967.

Gibaldi, Joseph. *MLA Handbook for Writers of Research Papers*. 6th ed. New York: Modern Language Association of America, 2003.

Judd, Karen. *Copyediting: A Practical Guide*. 3rd ed. Los Altos, CA: Crisp, 2001.

Lester, James D. *Writing Research Papers: A Complete Guide*. 10th ed. New York: Longman, 2001.

Martinich, A. P. *Philosophical Writing: An Introduction*. 3rd ed. London: Blackwell, 2005.

Matson, Wallace I. *A New History of Philosophy*. 2 vols. Belmont, CA: Wadsworth, 1999.

Rosenberg, Jay F. *The Practice of Philosophy*. 3rd ed. Upper Saddle River, NJ: Prentice-Hall, 1995.

Rosnow, Ralph L., and Mimi Rosnow. *Writing Papers in Psychology*. 7th ed. Belmont, CA: Wadsworth, 2005.

Roth, Audrey J. *The Research Paper: Process, Form, and Content*. 8th ed. Belmont, CA: Wadsworth, 1999.

Seech, Zachary. *Logic in Everyday Life: Practical Reasoning Skills*. Belmont, CA: Wadsworth, 1988.

———. *Open Minds and Everyday Reasoning*. 2nd ed. Belmont, CA: Wadsworth, 2004.

Strunk, William, Jr., and E. B. White. *Elements of Style*. 4th ed. New York: Longman, 2000.

Turabian, Kate L. *A Manual for Writers of Term Papers, Theses, and Dissertations*. 7th ed. Chicago: University of Chicago Press, 2007.

———. *Student's Guide for Writing College Papers*. Chicago: University of Chicago Press, 1977.

Weston, Anthony. *A Rulebook for Arguments*. 3rd ed. Indianapolis: Hackett, 2001.

Woodhouse, Mark B. *A Preface to Philosophy*. 8th ed. Belmont, CA: Wadsworth, 2006.

Index